Faithful of C

Robert Crighton in 1854

At the time of 'the awful occasion which showed the world how ignorant it was till then of one of its really greatest men'.

(*Glasgow Herald* March 10th 1854 quoting a New York newspaper.)

Faithful of Days

The Story of Robert Crighton
Master Mariner

Clare Abbott

YOUCAXTON PUBLICATIONS

OXFORD & SHREWSBURY

for Alan Boyd,

one of Robert Crighton's great, great grandsons

Also in memory of my father, Robert Burton Wight (1914-2003)
and grandfather, Henry Dewar Wight (1871-1961),
who designed the electrical systems of many great ships.

Preface

Surrounded by the sea, it is hardly surprising that we British children born in Twentieth Century Britain remember our history lessons peppered with the swashbuckling heroes who defended these shores against foreign invaders. But our Nelsons, Raleighs and Drakes were commanders of fighting ships, and their bravery was expressed in deeds against the men-of-war of other nations. Theirs was more a story of 'Rule Britannia' than one of ruling the waves. But there was another dimension to early seafaring and men had to pit their wits and skill against the worst that nature could devise. They needed courage and resourcefulness in command and an understanding of the frailties of others when disaster struck. The sea is a dangerous and unpredictable place. Those choosing a seafaring life entered a lottery where only strong leadership and experience might change the odds just a little in favour of survival.

Victorian Britain needed such men in their thousands to carry on the trade that fuelled a vast and ever-expanding commercial Empire. This book tells the story of one of them, an exceptional mariner who saved the lives of nearly two hundred men, women and children during a 'perfect storm' that raged in the West Atlantic for ten days over Christmas and New Year, 1853/4. Around this incident, Clare Abbott has built a picture of the life and character of Captain Robert Crighton of Port Glasgow. She has pieced together information from many sources and, with a forensic eye, has teased out the real man and his story from a jumble of (sometimes) contradictory evidence and journalistic mythology. Fortunately for my great-great-grandfather, his heroism was recognised at the time and this was to have a profound effect on the rest of his life. Adulation and honours came from all quarters, from the President of the United States down, but memories soon fade and for most of the time since his death he has all but been forgotten.

Clare has done a fine job in blowing the dust off Robert Crighton's story. I am immensely proud to be his descendant and grateful that such a skilled researcher has chosen to apply her talents to leading him out into the sunshine again. This book is also a tribute to the many brave mariners whose stories can never be told because they were not recorded.

Alan Boyd
Bath, Somerset, 2014

Acknowledgements

Jim Bell has very generously shared his fund of information over the years. He found many of the musical tributes and provided the splendid portrait of Robert in 1854.

Contributors to the Mariner's Message Board have been most helpful, especially Peter Klein, Paul Benyon and Piers Smith-Cresswell.

Betty Hendry of the Watt Library, Greenock answered several queries and Charlotte Cowe, genealogist, sent a vital document while kindly leaving me to discover the connection between Robert and Adam therein for myself.

Other librarians who went the extra mile are Hilde Laenen of Antwerp Public Library, Meg Gers of the Enoch Pratt Free Library, Baltimore and Ted Jackson of Georgetown University Library. Roger Hull of the Liverpool Record Office looked up references to Robert in several directories.

Rufus Boyd managed to winkle copies of the 'Ulster Link' articles from an Australian library after all my attempts had failed. Alexander M. Crighton's family in America supplied information about his life on Grand Cayman and Timothy D. A. Crighton alerted me to the fact that Robert's son Alexander had also rescued people from sinking ships. Keith Hannay did some sleuthing in Edinburgh.

Robert J. Chandler copied the beautiful drawings he owns of the *San Francisco's* engines and paddle wheel, encouraged me to include the Currer print and patiently educated me about bills of exchange. I am very grateful to Christine Reich for taking such splendid photographs of Robert's awards and to Dick Arch who photographed the memorials in the cemetery at Spotts.

Even though Lucia Eaton can no longer be thanked, her narrative gives a unique insight into what it was like to live through the tragedy and subsequent rescue on the *Kilby*.

Robert Fowke, friend and co-founder of YouCaxton and editor of this book, cajoled me into writing it properly and provided considerable support.

Above all, I am grateful to Alan Boyd for the opportunity to pursue this fascinating story and for his unfailing encouragement and enthusiasm in spite of the blind alleys and my occasional assertion that 'no more can be found'. I hope that plenty more *will* now be found. Alan also did some of the research (especially in Antwerp) and made the map of the rescue.

Thank you, everyone.

Contents

Preface	vii
Acknowledgements	ix
Illustrations	xii
Introduction	xiii
The Beginning	1
Early Ships	9
The Captain	15
The *San Francisco* Tragedy	27
On Board the Rescue Ships	45
Aftermath in America	56
The *Tornado* Years	70
The *John Bell*	97
Govan, Liverpool and the Last Commands	104
Antwerp	112
A Personal View of Robert	119
Robert and Jane's Descendants	125
Alexander and Margaret, Robert's Brother and Sister	131
Robert's Crighton Ancestors	138
Adam, Robert and Jeannie	150
Awards and Other Tributes	159
The Court of Inquiry	173
Robert's Financial Affairs	186
The Three Bells	190
List of Robert's Ships	192
Endnotes and References	194
Bibliography	209
Picture Credits	211
About the Author	212
Index	213

Illustrations

Frontispiece.

Robert Crighton in 1854

1. Port Glasgow in 1825, J.H.Clark   4
2. Robert's baptism from the Parish Register, 1821   5
3. List of the ships on which Robert served prior to getting his Master's Certificate, in his handwriting, 1855   11
4. Portrait of Jane Crighton. Oil; date and artist unknown   24
5. Drawing of one of the *San Francisco's* engines, 1854. F. Mone   28
6. Drawing of part of a paddle wheel of the *San Francisco*, 1854. F. Mone   29
7. *Glasgow Herald* November 21st 1853   30
8. The *Three Bells*. Lithograph published by Metzler and Co   31
9. The San Francisco Tragedy. Lithograph by N. Currer, painted by T. Butterworth, 1854   42
10. Map of the San Francisco tragedy. The ships are shown at known co-ordinates, except the *Kilby*, whose position when she left the area of the wreck has been estimated. Drawn by Alan Boyd   43
11. Gold snuff box from the City of New York   66
12. Portrait of Robert. Oil; date and artist unknown   109
13. Photograph of Robert as an old man   115
14. Overstamped Spanish coin   156
15. Gold medal from the merchants of New York   160

Introduction

With a few exceptions, mostly military, those once fêted for their outstanding bravery are soon forgotten and of civilians who risked their lives saving others from a watery grave, only the great Victorian heroine Grace Darling is generally remembered. Helen Petrie, who a few years later was prepared to row alone through mountainous seas to rescue two men clinging to an upturned boat, is now almost unknown. Just thirty years ago Andrew Parker, a passenger on the sinking *Herald of Free Enterprise*, used his body as a bridge over which twenty people crawled to safety and in 1951 Kenneth Dancy jumped between his ship and the heavily listing *Flying Enterprise* because he could see that the only man left on board, her captain Kurt Carlsen, would never be able to secure the vital tow rope unaided[2]. How many people can recall the names of these extraordinarily courageous men today?

This is the story of Captain Robert Crighton, the man Walt Whitman chose to represent all heroes. The hundreds[3] saved from the wreck of the *San Francisco* by his endeavours ensured that the name of their rescuer was honoured throughout the United States. His message of hope to those on the stricken vessel, 'Be of good cheer, we will not desert you' seems to have particularly caught the public imagination; most Americans reading Walt Whitman's poem when it was first published would have known who wrote those words and that Robert's ship the *Three Bells* stood by the helpless *San Francisco* for four long days and nights in the worst storm of the century, saving the lives of 185 people. Afterwards he would admit only to doing his duty and we might possibly agree, except that the *Three Bells* was leaking furiously, had few remaining provisions and had lost most of her sails. The United States Government did not agree either, since they awarded him their highest honour.

Robert's return to Scotland was barely noticed and to this day there is no acknowledgement of him in his birthplace of Port Glasgow. Modest in life, he has simply been forgotten there; his name does not appear in a recently published history of the town, not even in the chapter headed 'Famous People'[4].

It is difficult to imagine a world without instant communication, but at the time of the disaster it was not possible to radio from a ship for help. Telegraphy was in its infancy, though the captains of two vessels who 'passed by on the other side' could transmit details of the *San Francisco*'s position to New York when they reached port. The latest news from the United Kingdom was three months old by the time the newspapers and letters conveying it reached Australia.

An ancestor of mine went to the Gold Coast (now Ghana) in the late Eighteenth Century and married an African princess. He had to return to England without her – via America on a slave ship – and did not learn of the birth of their son for *years*.

My interest in Robert Crighton began several years ago when I attended a course tutored by Alan Boyd. During a coffee break I mentioned my hobby of family history. Alan wondered if more could be discovered about his ancestor, a ship's captain who had taken part in a famous rescue. I began to research the story almost immediately, helped by the many American newspapers published at the time and a diary of one of the survivors. I was delighted to discover that Robert once lived a short distance from my birthplace, near Tranmere Rover's football ground in Birkenhead. He must have travelled to his Liverpool office on the ferry across the River Mersey, as I did for too long on my reluctant way to school.

Robert always spelled his surname Crighton, but where Creighton was used I have retained that (including, somewhat disgracefully, on his Congressional Medal.) His father and grandfather used the Crighton spelling; his brother's descendants in America are usually Creighton.

Any family's history is a jigsaw with plenty of missing pieces. There are some unanswered questions about Robert's life: did he receive the money collected for him in America and, if so, what did he do with it? Why did he give up the sea for several years on two occasions and where are the majority of the medals he was awarded? The answers may never be found and the time has come to stop making excuses and to share my discoveries before I too become a document in a filing cabinet.

Clare Abbott
Oxford, 2014

Chapter One
The Beginning

Above the noise of the storm the sound of gunfire reverberated through the stricken ship, waking everyone who could still respond. Another vessel had been sighted! Some on board were too exhausted or despairing to care and for several cholera sufferers help would be too late, but others climbed the slippery companionways up to the dark, heaving deck, hardly daring to hope that this time they might be rescued. Loud cheers broke out when, sometimes, a light could be seen shining through gaps in the waves. The guns continued to sound for the rest of the night, keeping the ships in contact.

As dawn broke, the cold and anxious watchers on the wreck of the *San Francisco* saw the light draw closer, growing faint as the darkness receded. Just as it seemed there must be a collision with the ship that carried it, she was skilfully brought round and they could see the name *Three Bells* painted on her bow. No shouted words could be made out over the fury of the wind and the wild sea. Someone wrote a note, wrapped the paper round a weight and threw it towards the *Three Bells*. The first attempt failed but a second note landed safely and was immediately taken to a tall man standing on the deck, who was clearly her captain.

Robert Crighton read the message with disbelief and some disgust; it asked him to name his terms for rescuing everyone from the wreck.

'What does the man mean?' he demanded 'It's not money I'm after – I'm stopping for humanity's sake.'

But the meaning was perfectly clear and there were good grounds to fear that there might be no rescue. Two ships had already promised aid but sailed away and a third had only been able to take off about a hundred survivors. There were urgent reasons why Robert might have considered abandoning the *San Francisco*: his crew were exhausted from bailing round the clock, food and water were rationed and the *Three Bells* had only two sails remaining. Also, the sea was far too rough to begin the transfer immediately and much of his cargo would have to be dumped to accommodate so many extra people. The prudent course would have been to make for the nearest port and send help, though it would probably arrive too late. Fortunately for the survivors on the *San Francisco,* one of Walt Whitman's 'large hearts' was beating within Robert's chest and he would go down rather than sail away from the desperate people he could see lining the opposite deck.

This was probably more than most captains then or since would do 'for humanity's sake'. Recent times have seen the duty to assist made part of U.S Maritime Law, and the United Nations Convention of the Law of the Sea (1982) has the same compulsion 'as long as such action may reasonably be expected.' But aid between mariners (when not fighting each other!) is as old as sea-going itself. First promulgated by Eleanor of Aquitaine (the wife of Louis VII and then Henry II) in the Twelfth Century, the Rules or Laws of Oléron were based on even earlier codes. They enshrined the principle of aiding wrecked merchant sailors, though the main concern was the ship's cargo. These Laws were incorporated into the late mediaeval *Black Book of the Admiralty*, amplified and reprinted many times since[5]. During the European wars of the late Eighteenth and early Nineteenth Centuries, merchant ships sailed in convoys for safety and mutual help. Officers and crew of a ship in trouble often had previous shipmates on other vessels in the same convoy who came to their aid even in the severe conditions of the South Pacific, but only if the safety of their ship was not compromised. The opprobrium heaped on Captain Stanley Lord after he ignored the rocket signals from the *Titanic* suggests that by 1912 it was certainly expected that a merchant ship would help another in distress.

The essence of Robert's heroism was not only that he stayed

beside the *San Francisco* for four days when he might have been sailing towards safety, but that he did so even though the chances of success were not very high. Although in the very prime of life, recently married and with a child, Robert simply could not abandon hundreds of other men, women and children to their fate, even those suffering from cholera.

The story of this exceptional man begins in Scotland.

In 1831, two brothers were playing round some bollards on the south side of the River Clyde at a place called Port Glasgow. The view across the wide river was obscured by rows of sailing ships tied up alongside each other, but glimpses of the green fields of Dunbartonshire could sometimes be seen. Behind the quay were the crowded houses and filthy streets of the town which the boys, Robert Crighton and his brother Alexander, would leave for a life at sea.

Port Glasgow, then called Newark, was originally a fishing village on the River Clyde, twenty miles upstream of the great port of Glasgow. It was just a castle and a few cottages, surrounded by plum, pear and apple trees, clinging to a narrow strip of land between cliff and river. But by the late Eighteenth Century the Clyde had become so silted up that only ships with a shallow draught could reach Glasgow and, in 1774, Newark became Port Glasgow where facilities were built for large vessels. Their cargoes were redistributed among the smaller ships that were able to navigate up the Clyde to Glasgow itself[6].

Little is left from that time except a row of bollards where the two boys played, now slightly inland but still an eloquent testament to the many ships once tied up to them. It is easy to imagine old sailors sitting there, spinning horrifying or fascinating tales to any child who would listen. In reality, Robert and Alexander would not have had much time for games or stories, because their father died when they were only seven and six years old. This had not meant destitution (as the loss of a breadwinner often did), because the

Crighton family owned the building where they lived above their grocery shop. The boy's mother, Jeannie, continued the business and would have needed their help when not at school. Education was not compulsory at the time, but the brothers had reasonably good handwriting and later passed navigation examinations, which required mathematics. They may even have attended the one school (of eight) in Port Glasgow where navigation was taught[7].

1. Port Glasgow in 1825, J.H.Clark

There was always work to do in a grocery. Sugar was delivered in large conical 'loaves', each weighing about six kilos which had to be cut up using 'sugar nips', like heavy pliers but with sharp edges. Oats, potatoes, dried peas and flour were bought in bulk and required weighing out and bagging. Muslin-wrapped bacon hung in large pieces from hooks on the ceiling, reached down and sliced for each customer. Alcohol was sold in earthenware containers which were refilled many times until they were too chipped or cracked to be used again. There were heavy sacks to move around, deliveries to make and the premises to be kept clean. Shops were open for fourteen to sixteen hours a day and until 10 pm on Saturday. All closed on the Sabbath, when no play was permitted and two church services with long sermons were attended by many. Best clothes were worn and had to be kept clean[8].

Most children did quite heavy domestic duties as soon as they were strong enough – carrying water, emptying the waste and tending fires. Food was usually cooked on an open hearth in the early Nineteenth Century. In Scotland bannocks (oat or barley flat breads) were baked on a metal plate smeared with mutton fat and suspended over the fire.

Robert Crighton was born on May 5th 1821, the eldest child of Jeannie (baptised Jane) McKeich and Robert Crighton senior who were married in 1818. Scottish women kept their maiden names

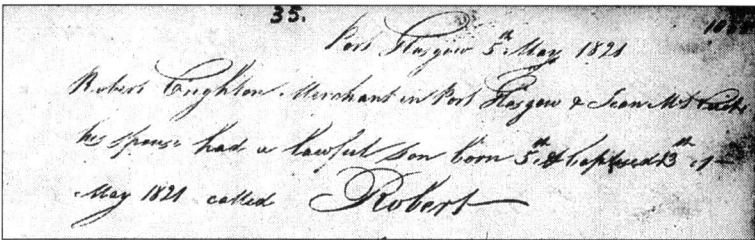

2. Robert's Baptism from the Parish Register, 1821

throughout life; in legal documents[9] Jeannie was referred to as 'Jean or Jane McKeich, Mrs. Crighton'. Alexander was born in 1822, Margaret in 1825 and baby Jeanie in 1828, though she did not long survive baptism. With them lived Robert senior's widowed sister Janet and her two girls, his disabled brother Adam and his parents Adam and Janet, although Robert junior would not have been able to remember his grandfather who died before he was two. Grandmother Janet outlived her husband, but it is not known for how long because there are no Port Glasgow burial records for the time. Civil registration did not begin in Scotland until 1855.

Very little is left of the town Robert knew. The house where he was born, at the corner of King Street and Lyon's Lane, vanished long ago and even the lane itself no longer exists. Newark Castle however, once home to the Maxwell family and dating from 1478, still stands[10].

Robert would also recognise the fine Town Buildings of 1816, the Kirk of 1823 and the oldest (1758) purpose-built Masonic Lodge in the world at 9-11½ King Street. This odd 'half' numbering of houses appears to be unique to Port Glasgow and that address also contained the Corporation school. All the other buildings from the time of Robert's childhood have been demolished[11].

Port Glasgow had the first dry dock in Europe and a wet dock was taking shape when Robert went to sea. The Corporation had borrowed more than £25,000 to finance this grand venture, which should have greatly increased trade. Unfortunately the new dock was built directly onto shifting silt and the wall on the seaward side collapsed almost immediately. The town was already using half its annual income of just under £2000 to pay the interest on a previous loan and was now bankrupt. As a result of this disaster, Port Glasgow had to 'observe strict financial economy for the rest of the century or it may never have recovered'[12].

The town's chief industries in Robert's time were shipbuilding, sugar refining and rope and sail making; the main imports were tobacco (mostly from America), sugar and rum (from the West Indies), brandy, wine and salt, and especially timber (from North America and Europe), of which 27,925 tons arrived in 1834.

In 1831, when Robert was ten years old, the population of Port Glasgow was 4,192[13], crowded on the same narrow strip between the cliffs and the river where there had once been a single row of cottages. Most houses were very cold in winter and had no water supply – only seventeen of the wealthiest households had a private tap; everyone else collected water from wells or from public taps fed by a reservoir. The Public Baths and Washhouse did not open until 1894. Clothes were generally washed in the river, especially at a place where warm water entered from one of the sugar refining factories. There was no indoor sanitation, just a bucket emptied into one of the middens in the street. The Clyde carried all the waste from Glasgow past the port – the campaign to ship the city's sewage to the Ayrshire coast did not start until 1835 – and the stench was appalling, especially in summer[14].

Gas came to Port Glasgow in 1829 but only lit the rooms of the rich. It cost nine shillings per light per year up to 8 pm and twenty-two shillings for three further hours; checks were made, even to the extent that the inspectors entered houses to feel if the gas mantles were warm when unpaid-for use was suspected[15]. Most people could only afford the glimmer of a tallow dip – a strip of burning cloth in a saucer of animal fat. Slightly more expensive were tallow candles or an oil lamp, usually burning fish oil. All these gave off an unpleasant smell. Wax from bees and some plants was very expensive and paraffin wax was not made in commercial quantities until the mid-Nineteenth Century.

For most people, transport was by foot, boat or hired horse and cart; only a few could afford a horse-drawn carriage. The railway came in 1841, causing the destruction of some dwellings and many of the orchards.

Port Glasgow had eighty-one public houses in 1831, forty-five spirit dealers and twelve grocers who also sold spirits, including the Crightons. There must have been considerable drunkenness, but in spite of this only two men were in prison that year for serious crimes. There were five butchers, three hatters and two booksellers' shops, but no dairy or fishmonger[16]. A herd of goats lived in the town, whose owner would milk one for a halfpenny and, until the late Eighteenth Century, pigs freely roamed the streets.

Robert and Alexander would have worn versions of adult clothes, perhaps a jacket and collarless shirt with a necktie, rough trousers, thick socks and boots. Several paintings by Scottish artists of the period[17] and photographs of young prisoners in Newcastle a little later show similar clothing.

In 1835, fourteen-year-old Robert was apprenticed to the merchant service. Why did he and Alexander turn their backs on a thriving family business and venture into the harsh and dangerous world of sailing ships? They could have been under no illusions about the reality of life at sea; the scars and missing limbs of the old sailors they had seen all their lives would have been witness to that. Perhaps they wanted to escape the monotony of a shopkeeper's life, or maybe they simply felt:

> *'the call of the running tide*
> *Is a wild call and a clear call that may not be denied'*

(John Masefield, *Sea Fever*)

Chapter Two

Early Ships

The crew of a merchant sailing ship was made up of able (to hand, reef and steer)[18] and ordinary seamen led by the boatswain, all under the control of the officers. These were the first and second mates (more on a large vessel) who received their orders from the captain, sometimes referred to as a 'master under God', answerable to the ship's owners for a fast and profitable voyage. The safety of everyone on board depended on the skill and knowledge of their captain, while his personality determined the everyday lives of the crew.

The men were divided into two watches, each under the supervision of one of the mates. A watch was four hours long except between four and eight pm, when there were two of half that. The ship's bell measured out the time, being struck once at the end of the first half hour, twice on the hour, and so on until it was struck eight times signalling the end of the watch (unless it was late afternoon). Observations of the ship's speed and direction were taken several times during the day and night to aid navigation, which was the master's responsibility.

There were some specialised members of the crew: a carpenter, sailmaker and cook, with a surgeon on larger ships. Otherwise the captain administered medicine and performed minor surgery such as pulling teeth and lancing boils; for more serious conditions he could seek help from other ships or in port. Sometimes sailors were left in a foreign hospital with their possessions, to make their own way home if they survived.

The path to becoming a ship's officer was via an apprenticeship. After 1823, all merchant ships over eighty tons were required to carry apprentices but there was no legislation concerning their welfare or that of any other crew member[19]. The captain alone determined the sleeping and working conditions of his crew: what they ate and drank and how they were disciplined. A further Act, passed in 1850, made nine superficial feet of sleeping space for each man compulsory, also the provision of medicines (but no physician or instruction book). However, these laws were rarely, if ever, enforced.

The food on board was not very palatable. Salty, tough and fatty pork or beef that had been preserved in barrels was soaked and then boiled in sea water, served on ship's biscuit or hashed with potatoes and onions. Some ships carried chickens and even pigs to provide fresh food but this was only rarely for the crew. Dried pulses were made into soup and tea was brewed very strongly. Each man had an allowance of flour which was made into bread or 'duff', a kind of pudding with a few raisins and perhaps molasses. The food stores were infested with insects (prompting jokes about choosing the lesser of two weevils)[20] and eaten by the inevitable rats[21]. Cats and even dogs reduced the vermin but could not eliminate them. Fishing was not very successful while the ship was moving, but any flying fish that landed on the decks were a welcome addition to the diet. If the captain's wife was on board, she was traditionally offered these fish.

Apprentices were bound for a set number of years, usually four. In theory they were instructed in seamanship, navigation and the duties of deck officers in return for food, accommodation and any pay as agreed. Unfortunately, many captains regarded apprentices as cheap labour and ignored their training. In 1833 a commission was set up to examine the state of the mercantile marine and reported that 'the British Merchant service is populated by drunken and incompetent shipmasters, some of whom could not navigate using a sextant and chronometer'[22].

Robert (or his mother, who would have signed the indentures) chose a good ship, the *Leguan*, in which to learn his trade[23]. Fourteen was not particularly young to go to sea – midshipmen entered the

3. List of the ships on which Robert served
prior to getting his Master's Certificate,
in his handwriting, 1855

Royal Navy aged eleven or twelve and could then face enemy fire.
Many children started work even earlier. In 1842 four year olds were
found operating the trap doors in coal mines, alone and in the dark;
at six they started to pull heavy trucks[24].

The *Leguan* was built in Port Glasgow in 1828 and plied between
the Clyde and Demerara, returning with sugar, rum and molasses
produced by slaves. Leguan is an island off the coast of Demerara, now
part of Guyana, the only English speaking country in South America.
Slave trading had been abolished in 1807, but slavery itself was not
made illegal in British colonies until the Abolition Act of 1833[25].

Robert began his apprenticeship on November 5th, 1835. Arrivals
and departures of British merchant ships were recorded in local and
national newspapers, but the coverage was far from complete. Few
of the *Leguan*'s voyages appear, but one[26] shows her departing from
Demerara on August 30th 1836 in company with the *Louisa*, arriving at
Port Glasgow on October 22nd. A round trip took about four months.

Many years after Robert left the ship, the end of the *Leguan* in 1860 was spectacular. She survived a stormy night off the west coast of Ireland after losing an anchor and without her masts, which had been chopped down for stability. While the captain was ashore organising replacements, a fire started in the hold. The crew almost swamped the rowing boats in their haste to get away, without making any effort to put out the fire – and who can blame them? The rum casks exploded, sheets of flame lit up the sky and eventually the *Leguan* sank. 'There is no allegation that the fire could have arisen from spontaneous combustion and no explanation is offered by the crew who are said to have been on bad terms with the captain'[27].

During Robert's apprenticeship, King William IV died and Queen Victoria (1837-1901) started her long reign. At the end of the four years he joined the *Helen Hamilton* of Liverpool as second mate, in charge of one of the watches and learning how to control the crew. The *Helen Hamilton* traded with Venezuela, whose chief exports in the 1840s were coffee and the very finest cocoa. She left Liverpool on July 23rd 1840 for La Guayra, Puerto Cabello and Maracaibo and set off on the return journey on November 1st with Robert as first mate. This was rapid promotion indeed (perhaps the original first mate died), a testimonial to his good training on the *Leguan*. Robert was now second in command, controlling one of the watches, being the captain's eyes and ears and taking over if the latter died or became incapacitated. The *Helen Hamilton* reached Liverpool on January 3rd 1841.

The ship was cleared outwards again on February 3rd 1841 and returned on May 7th with a rather unusual item in her hold. The forty barrels and eleven casks of *Balsam capivi* (a tree resin used in medicine and varnishes) were later auctioned[28].

Robert had one further voyage in the *Helen Hamilton* and left her in Liverpool on October 10th 1841. His career was going well; he had risen in rank and the risks, although considerable, could have been worse. During this time the First Anglo-Afghan (1839-1842) war was fought 'for no wise purpose, carried on with a strange mixture of rashness and timidity… not one benefit, political or military, was acquired'[29]. Almost all the 16,500 British and Indian soldiers and camp followers who withdrew from Kabul in 1842 died in the snowbound mountain passes on their way to Jalalabad.

In October 1841 Robert joined the barque *Cingalese* as first mate. She sailed from Liverpool to Montevideo, the capital of Uruguay, whose chief exports were leather, wool and meat. One newspaper reported her return to Liverpool from Montevideo on November 4th 1842; another says she had left from Buenos Ayres[30]. The latter city had been the scene of a massacre earlier that year, when hundreds of people were killed simply for belonging to the wrong political party. Those who could do so fled to Montevideo, on the other side of the River Plate[31].

The next voyage of the *Cingalese* took Robert to the Far East. He was in Indonesia by June:

Batavia, June 8th 1843
The Cingalese (Hutchison) from the Clyde to this port, ran aground at Man Eater's Island on June 3rd but has been assisted off apparently without damage after discharging part of her cargo, and towed to the Roads[32].

Man Eater's Island is at the end of a long sandbar extending into the Indian Ocean from Java. If there were hungry tigers about, perhaps it is fortunate that the crew did not have to abandon ship.

Batavia (now Jakarta) was built on marshy ground with a network of canals – evil-smelling open sewers 'infested with alligators and venomous reptiles.' Although described in 1787[33] as a 'superb and magnificent city,' it was a very unhealthy place for Europeans because the large, brackish-water fish ponds constructed in the mid-

Eighteenth Century were ideal breeding places for mosquitoes[34]. Foreigners contracted 'Java Disease' (malaria) to which the local people eventually acquired some immunity. Until treatment with quinine was introduced in the mid-Nineteenth Century, malaria was frequently fatal and survivors usually suffered from periodic relapses of 'shaking fever' for years afterwards.

After leaving Batavia, the *Cingalese* sailed for Singapore, a vital link in the trade between Britain and China. Before Sir Stamford Raffles secured the right to establish a trading post there in 1819, the Dutch controlled trade in the Malay Archipelago. Spices were the chief export of the area, but tariffs were high[35]. The far-sighted Raffles made Singapore a free port (without taxes or dues) and by the late 1840s Britain dominated trade in the Far East. In 1851 the Horsburgh Lighthouse was built at the entrance to the Straits of Singapore, named for the famous hydrographer James Horsburgh (1762-1836) whose charts of the Indo-Chinese seas saved the lives of many sailors.

The *Cingalese* left Singapore at the end of September, 1843, arrived at the Cape of Good Hope in early December, was at Deal on February 10th and entered inwards at London three days later, where Robert left her.

Chapter Three
The Captain

'It is no small charge, that of Master of a ship trading round the world'
(Hilary Marquand[36])

1843 saw the first major shipping slump of the Nineteenth Century in the United Kingdom[37], which ended when guano was discovered on islands off the west coasts of South America and Africa. This is the waste that accumulates where birds or bats congregate, valuable both as a fertilizer and in the manufacture of explosives. The Incas had used guano (and controlled its collection) for centuries but did not enlighten their Spanish conquerors about its properties.

The rush to collect this 'white gold' gave Robert his great opportunity. At the age of only twenty-two he secured his first command, of the barque *Roscanna* which left Liverpool in April 1844 bound for Angra Pequena, a coastal area in the south of Namibia. Captain Morrell had landed on Ichaboe, a nearby island, in 1828 and reported 'bird's manure' twenty-five feet deep. First trialled in Liverpool in 1835, guano was imported in commercial quantities from 1840. It was a very unpleasant cargo, giving off ammonia and covering the ship with irritating dust. Loading conditions were appalling – men could only work in the hold for five minutes at a time, with rope round their waists in case they passed out. Guano was also a considerable fire hazard.

Ichaboe was a harsh environment in which to work[38]. Home for the labourers was a rough wooden shelter or often just a sail held up by old casks, with no fire because there was little fuel. Fresh water was limited and usually contaminated with salt; the food was unpalatable and lacking fruit or vegetables. Irritation from the dust caused bleeding from the nose and eyes, alcohol was limited and there were no recreational or medical facilities at all on the island.

The men hacked at the guano with crowbars and pickaxes, shifted the lumps into wheelbarrows and took them to the landing stages where they were bagged for loading. This presented a problem. More ships arrived each day than could be loaded and a backlog developed. Without a harbour they had to anchor while awaiting their turn. The few landing stages were frequently destroyed by the weather and could take a week or more to rebuild, adding to the waiting time. Sailors (rather than the land labourers) had to do the loading and, in April 1844, they mutinied[39][40].

Sent by the Admiralty to deal with this situation, HMS *Thunderbolt* arrived in May, followed by HMS *Clio* and HMS *Isis*. New and unpopular rules for loading were imposed on crews and labourers. Two mutineers and one captain were transported to St Helena in irons for trial. The naval ships had left by July when the recalcitrants rebelled again, denying the shipmasters access to the island and increasing the price of guano. 'The utmost possible anarchy reigned among the crews of the numerous vessels lying there [and the anchorage was] very unsafe owing to the little shelter and bad holding ground mostly rocky and uneven. On June 29th there was a severe gale and heavy seas... some ships slipped their anchors. The nights became cold and damp, the dew falling from the rigging like rain.'[41] (Captain Tasker of the brig *Leila*)

Ships continued to arrive at Ichaboe, sometimes thirty in a week, and had to anchor where they could. Captain Hancock of the *Victoria* was horrified[42]:

There are 70-80 vessels here getting athwart hawse of the other. Really this is a very serious state of affairs. 70-80 ship's crews in mutiny at such a place as this. If our countrymen cannot load their ships without fighting, how will it be when the foreigners

arrive ? [the French were rumoured] It is to be hoped the
Admiralty will do something for the protection of the island. A
man of war would always have the assistance of the respectable
shipmasters.

These extraordinarily difficult conditions continued until December
1844 when HMS *Thunderbolt* returned. Among the 'respectable
shipmasters' waiting for their freight was Robert. The *Roseanna* appears
in a list of about a hundred and twenty ships anchored at Ichaboe
on August 11th, 1844[43]. Robert found himself competing for loading
space with other British captains in an atmosphere of antagonism
and resentment. He had to get his men to load other ships so that the
Roseanna would eventually be loaded in turn and also had to pay an
inflated price for the guano. Having a captive market, the suppliers of
food and water probably increased their prices as well.

There was a terrific storm on the return journey:

Arrived in the Clyde on Friday, the barque Roseanna (397)
of Greenock, Crichton, from Ichaboe in 103 days, sailed 30th
September with a cargo of guano. Called at Cork for orders and
sailed again for the Clyde on 11th ult, was subsequently blown
down Channel as far as lat 15 with heavy gales of wind; being
unable to come South, bore up for the North Channel, and after
getting to Tory Island, was blown off as far as Barrahead[44].

Tory Island is off the north-west coast of County Donegal, Ireland,
and Barra Head is the southernmost point of the Outer Hebrides. Some
repairs were necessary after this storm and the ship was then sold[45].

Robert stayed with the *Roseanna* and the new owner(s) sent her to
China, where trade had recently been interrupted by the First Opium
War (1839-1842). This sprang from Britain's insatiable demand for
tea, for which the Chinese would only accept payment in silver[46].

The result was a huge and growing trade deficit and a shortage of the metal in Britain. The East India Company (which had a monopoly on the tea trade) developed a 'solution': by 1817 opium grown in India was sent to China in Company ships. But this ingenious new import was banned by the Chinese authorities, although bribery and the tax collected on extra tea sales meant that it was tolerated for a while[47]. The number of opium addicts increased so alarmingly that in 1839 the Chinese made importation of the drug punishable by death and British merchants in Canton had their stock burned outside their warehouses. To this day, Chinese schoolchildren are taught what the British did to their country. In spite of opposition from those who despised the opium trade, the British Prime Minister Lord Palmerston, 'a man who misunderstood the world – especially the Orient'[48] sent an expeditionary force that inflicted a humiliating defeat on the Chinese. By the Treaty of Nanking of 1842, five Chinese ports were opened to foreign trade and Britain gained a new colony, the island of Hong Kong, where opium could be imported legally. Robert was able to take advantage of this new trading opportunity.

In 1839, Aden had also become a British colony, a centre for trade with the East and a coaling station for steamers. Transported in sailing ships, coal was a hazardous cargo because it shifted about and sometimes combusted spontaneously, this latter risk increasing with the length of the voyage[49].

Troon
Arrived here on Thursday evening last [March 6th 1845] from Greenock, the barque Roseanna in ballast, to load with coal for Aden. We are sorry to say that while the ship was being moved in the harbour, Malcolm McGeachy, one of the crew, unfortunately fell from the vessel and... struck the pier. He survived only about 16 hours. He was a respectable man of steady habits and is deeply regretted by the master and owners[50].

Ballast is carried if there is no cargo, to prevent a ship capsizing. It is usually something very cheap such as stones, sand or water.

Robert sailed on March 13th and by the summer had left Aden for Bombay (arrived August 28th) and then on to Madras, the chief loading port for opium. There were other possible cargoes that could be sold in China – cotton from India or tin and pepper from the Malay states – but opium was the most profitable. The *Roseanna* departed for Hong Kong on October 19th, crossing the pirate-infested South China Sea and probably armed with a pair of light cannons and a range of smaller weapons such as pistols, pikes and cutlasses. Anti-boarding nets were rigged at night but the pirates could overcome most defences and some ships, although with guard boats in attendance, even had the copper plates clandestinely removed from their hulls!

The most usual cargo on the return journey was tea although other exports from China included alum, musk, sago, silk, porcelain and ivory and wood carvings. The *Roseanna* left Hong Kong and sailed through the Strait of Sunda, between Java and Sumatra, on March 4th 1846. This was, and is, difficult to navigate because of strong tidal rips and shallow areas. Robert then crossed the Indian Ocean and rounded the dangerous Cape of Good Hope before arriving at St Helena on June 24th. The *Roseanna* reached Gravesend on August 24th and presumably sailed back to Scotland (her home port was Greenock at the time), though there is no record of her arrival.

Robert was in Port Glasgow in the early months of 1847. His mother died in January and in February he applied for and was granted his father's share of the King Street property. As an executor of his mother's will[51], he made an inventory of her possessions, listed her debtors and creditors and held a public sale of the stock remaining in the shop. Then he joined his next ship, the *Amelia*, at Dundee and sailed her to Greenock. He arrived on March 11th and later that day declared his mother's final financial position under oath before

James Lade, writer (solicitor) of Port Glasgow. Jeannie's will was proved at Paisley six days later.

The *Amelia* left the Clyde for Singapore on March 15th. Robert was likely to be away for a year and perhaps for much longer. His sister Margaret decided not to wait for his return and married James Thomson, a customs officer, in Port Glasgow on June 10th.

The ship must have encountered some stormy weather in the Atlantic:

The Amelia, Creighton, from Clyde for Singapore put into Rio [de] Janeiro May 4th with main mast sprung [cracked][52].

Pieces of wood called 'fish' (convex on one side and concave on the other) could be lashed round a damaged mast, but this was only a temporary measure. A proper repair was needed as soon as possible and Rio was on the usual route taken by ships sailing to the East Indies – they followed the trade winds, which meant heading for South America after stopping at say, Madeira, for provisions. Where they called next depended on health issues. Captains would sail as far south as the River Plate if the Brazilian ports were badly affected by malaria or yellow fever and then wait for the next trade wind to carry them across the South Atlantic towards the Cape of Good Hope[53].

It is difficult to follow Robert's journey because there were several ships called *Amelia* and newspaper reports did not always distinguish between them by including the captain's name. One definite sighting is that the *Mischief* 'spoke with' the *Amelia* October 29th 1847 on her way to Calcutta from Singapore. Ships flying flags of friendly countries often contacted (spoke with) each other at sea. This was an opportunity to exchange news, send letters and replenish medical or other supplies. Captains reported such interactions to the shipping office at the next suitable port. The information was then passed on to the press for publication, which provided reassurance for ship owners and the families of those on board.

The *Amelia* is listed as being at Singapore from Hong Kong in the *Caledonian Mercury* of November 29th 1847, but the news had probably taken several weeks to get to Scotland. The only other certain record shows her leaving Calcutta for China and Singapore on February 2nd 1848, which looks like a second voyage. There does not seem to be a notice of the *Amelia's* return to the Clyde, but Robert wrote (in his record of service) that he left the ship in October 1848. If this date is correct it was six months before he set sail again. His home base was Port Glasgow with his sister Margaret, her husband James and their baby Jeanie, which may be where he met his future wife, James's sister Jane Thomson. It was quite usual for women of the family to come and help around the time a baby was born, especially with the cooking and washing. Without plastic, non-iron fabrics or disposable nappies there was a great deal of laundry to be done, all by hand.

Robert next command was of the *Zarah* with his brother Alexander as second mate[54]. This was potentially a tricky situation – captains ate with their officers but could not be too familiar with them because discipline had to be maintained. The ship left in April 1849 bound for Batavia (for spices), returning via Bombay (for cotton, jute and indigo). After rounding the Cape of Good Hope they sailed to the small island of St Helena in the South Atlantic where supplies of water and provisions could be replenished, especially fruit and vegetables to prevent scurvy. The *Zarah* left St Helena for the Clyde in February 1850 and arrived on April 22nd. In May the *Glasgow Herald* carried a notice of a public auction of 'about twenty bales of cotton' from the *Zarah* and the *Cumberland* which had been damaged by sea water, suggesting they had been in some very stormy conditions.

There was a new baby, John, at King Street but Robert and Jane had only a few weeks together before the *Zarah* sailed again from

Clydeside in June 1850, this time without Alexander. The ship left Batavia for Singapore in October and was at Manila, capital of the Philippines (for sugar, tar, hemp, coconuts and resins) by the end of February 1851.

On the return journey Robert arrived at Queenstown (Cork) for orders on September 17th and reported his first rescue:

By the arrival off Queenstown of the Zarah from Manila we learn that about a month since she spoke with the brig Mozelle of this port [London] out 90 days from Africa, short of provisions and with part of her crew dead. She was supplied with provisions by the Zarah[55].

Many of her crew were still sick when the *Mozelle* got home but they had survived.

When the *Zarah* berthed in the Clyde on 24th September, Robert had some arrangements to make rather quickly. The Mercantile Marine Act of 1850 made it compulsory for captains of foreign-going ships to have a Certificate of Competency which, for new masters, meant passing written examinations[56]. Those who had commanded a ship before January 1st 1851 needed only a Certificate of Service. Robert applied for his on 9th October, listing his previous sea-going experience and giving the Port Glasgow address. The certificate was issued on October 27th.

Meanwhile he and Jane were married at Bervie, Kincardineshire on October 14th. They had been apart for eighteen months. Jane was with her parents and younger sister Katharine at Sillyflat Farm, Bervie (which still exists) on census night, March 1851, but had probably also stayed with Margaret and James in Port Glasgow, awaiting Robert's return and helping with the children.

The ship was due to sail again on November 10th but there was a ten day delay for repairs after the steamer *Glasgow* 'got in contact with the ship *Zarah* for Bombay and did some damage'[57]. This was on November 7th, so the *Zarah* was still moored but even if she had not been, the accident would have been the *Glasgow*'s fault because steam gives way to sail.

When the *Zarah* left the Clyde on November 17th bound for India and China, Jane went too. In the merchant service it was quite usual for captain's wives to accompany their husbands[58]. They shared his cabin in the stern of the ship and ate with the mates, who were not necessarily chosen for their fine manners. Time could hang heavily with no other women to talk to and some wives found the life very lonely. They did not associate with the crew and mostly stayed below decks. A few women (daughters and sisters as well as the wives of captains) learned navigation, a useful skill if the captain was sick, and some cooked. The galley was a male preserve but food could be prepared and sent there with instructions. Cakes, for example, were always welcome and could sometimes be exchanged with passing ships for fresh fruit or other luxuries.

In May 1852 the *Caledonian Mercury* reported that the *Zarah* had reached Bombay, but not on what date. She then sailed for Whampoa, China, which was the limit to which foreign vessels could go towards Canton. There a Chinese agent had to be hired to 'manage the needs of the ship and pay the customary bribes and taxes' while the ships waited at anchor. It was an unpleasant place in which to stay: hot, humid and with the ever-present threats of disease (especially typhus, transmitted by lice) and pirates. On the plus side their diet improved because families on sampans brought fresh vegetables and provisions and raised ducks to sell to those on board[59].

Jane's portrait radiates serenity, good humour and kindness. She was a brave woman to sail round the world knowing that she would be likely to have a child in the very public conditions of a sailing ship, thousands of miles from home and without the help of a midwife. Robert and Jane's daughter, also called Jane, was born at Whampoa

4. Portrait of Jane Crighton. Oil; date and artist unknown

in late 1852 or early 1853. Captains sometimes delivered their own children, but the *Zarah* was at a popular anchorage and it is more likely that women from other ships looked after mother and baby. Infants were sewn or tied into their nappies (which were washed by being towed behind the ship!) and into their beds at sea[60]. There had been plenty of time on the voyage for sewing and knitting baby clothes and perhaps the ship's carpenter made a cradle.

Trading finally completed and her new cargo stowed, the *Zarah* left China for Valparaiso in Chile – distance from Hong Kong, 10,450 miles.

Ships sometimes went southwards via Australia and New Zealand but there is no record of the *Zarah* calling there, so she probably headed straight across the Pacific Ocean via Hawaii. After Valparaiso they sailed down the west coast of South America and then faced the great hazard of Cape Horn, the graveyard of many sailors and one of the most feared passages in the world. A ship's surgeon who experienced it in 1871 wrote[61]:

> *The sea got like mountains rolling past the ship, which actually stopped against these awful waves. This was a dreadful sea and the vessel was almost lost in it, taking in large waves behind at the stern. My cabin…[was] floating full of water… everyone was in terror that she would not come through it.*

However unpleasant and terrifying it was for passengers, it was far worse for the sailors:[62]

> *Crew were ordered aloft to take in topsails. At that height above the water, movement was tremendous. Footropes were the only footholds and thick spars the only place for their hands when they were not at work on the sails. Both ropes and spars might be coated with ice; one slip meant death. The helmsman, waist deep in icy water, was lashed to his wheel throughout his watch.*

After Cape Horn, the *Zarah* crossed the Atlantic from south to north and from west to east, reaching Deal in Kent in fog on October 13th 1853, and 'proceeded for the River' (Thames). She berthed in London the next day. Two days later she entered outwards for Valparaiso, which was a very quick turnaround, sailed for Cardiff in November and was later reported at Buenos Ayres. Meanwhile, it seems that Robert and Jane made their own way to Glasgow with the baby and all their luggage, perhaps by train which took twelve-

and-a-half hours. They had been away for twenty-two months and sailed right round the world.

Robert was not at home for long. At the end of November he left the Clyde for New York in command of the *Three Bells*, reputedly the largest iron ship then afloat. This voyage had been advertised on November 7th with Campbell as master but something had occurred that demanded a replacement captain. Jane did not accompany him this time; she was expecting another child and Robert was likely to be away for only a few weeks.

Chapter Four

The *San Francisco* Tragedy

'Death chasing it up and down the storm'

In New York during the last few months of 1853 the stage was being set for a shipwreck that resulted in the greatest loss of life at sea yet recorded and such heroism that the United States was briefly set aflame. Intended for the Pacific Mail Service, the SS *San Francisco* was launched on 9th June. She had a wooden hull with bulkheads reinforced by double iron diagonal braces and two large paddle wheels powered by oscillating steam engines, each with a smokestack. There were also auxiliary sails with their associated (two) masts and rigging.

The *San Francisco*'s first sea trial – in calm water – ended ignominiously[63]. The condenser in the air-exhaust pump was of novel design and failed in an hour, causing loss of steam. Engineers twice modified it with the same result; each time the ship had to be towed back to her berth. This did not prevent her owners W.H.Aspinwall and Co. from tendering to take the Third Regiment of the United States Artillery from New York to California round Cape Horn, a journey of some thirteen thousand miles. They won the contract (worth $75,000) after considerable correspondence and delay. The regiment was going to the west to keep order in the goldfields; the officers could pay for their own overland transport if they preferred that to the long sea journey, the ordinary soldiers had no such choice.

The faulty condenser was removed (but not replaced), the paperwork signed and loading of the *San Francisco* begun. Coal was twenty-four dollars a ton cheaper in New York than in Rio de Janeiro, the first port

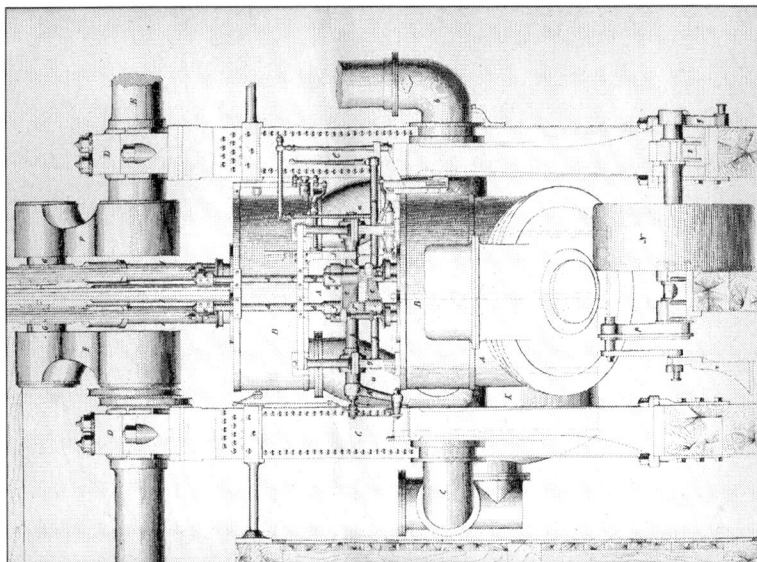

5. Drawing of one of the *San Francisco's* engines, 1854. F. Mone

of call, and so eight hundred tons were loaded which was far more than necessary to get to Brazil. There was an enormous amount of other cargo, including furniture, military equipment, twelve month's stores for the regiment and three for the crew, animals (cattle, sheep, pigs and poultry), their pens and fodder. A passenger wrote later that the ship was obviously overloaded, 'the paddle wheels had so much dip as to cause great strain upon her shaft and engines'.

Over seven hundred people added to this weight: five hundred or so military personnel with camp followers (wives, children, cooks, laundresses), some private passengers approved by the army and the ship's crew. The coal took up so much space that about three hundred soldiers were squashed into accommodation meant for two hundred and the rest had to sleep on deck. Most of these were in 'standee' canvas berths stacked three deep, which effectively suspended them in the icy wind. Some soldiers had to try to sleep on the paddle wheel guards and about fifteen were not allocated anywhere at all and lay down wherever they could find space. The army officers were assigned suites or cabins according to rank.

6. Drawing of part of a paddle wheel of the *San Francisco*, 1854. F. Mone

The private passengers included Mr G. Aspinwall, brother of the ship's owners, who was travelling to a drier climate for his health (he had tuberculosis), Lieutenant F. Murray of the US Navy and Captain Gardiner of the Light Dragoons. The *San Francisco* was commanded by Captain James T. Watkins who had previously been to the Far East and fought pirates, reputedly personally killing a dozen on one occasion[64]. The crew included a physician, Dr Buel, First Officer Edward Mellus and Chief Engineer John Marshall.

The *Three Bells* had set sail for New York on November 24th with twenty-four crew and sixteen passengers. Owned by three men with the surname Bell, she was built at Denny's yard in Dumbarton and launched in 1850.

NOTICE TO SHIPPERS.

Now rapidly proceeding with her Loading at Shed No. 31, South Side, and will be despatched pointedly on Thursday, 24th November.

FOR NEW YORK.

THE splendid A 1 at Lloyd's Clipper Ship THREE BELLS, 648 tons register, ROBT. CRICHTON, Commander.

To insure a *rapid* passage, the heavy freight taken has been limited; and from the noted character of this Ship as a remarkably fast sailer, a most favourable opportunity is here presented to Shippers of Fine Goods.

Shippers are respectfully requested to send down their Goods without delay.

For freight or passage, apply to

FINLAY BELL, 176 Argyll Street; or
JOHN ATHYA & CO., 10 Dixon Street.
Glasgow, 16th Nov., 1853.

Mate's Receipts required with Bills of Lading.

---

7. Glasgow Herald November 21st 1853[65]

The crew agreement[66] for this voyage included the condition that 'no spirits are allowed, and the crew engage to be on board sober, at the time stated, or the Master may ship others in their place.' This seems moderately draconian, but drunken officers were a menace at sea. Ordinary sailors were too poor to buy spirits and were probably more aggrieved at having to turn up sober the first morning! Nothing is specified about the return journey, except that it would be within six months of leaving Glasgow.

The provision list for the voyage specified a pound (about half a kilo) of bread, one-and-a-quarter or one-and-a-half pounds of meat, a ration of tea, coffee, sugar and three quarts of water (about three-and-a-quarter litres) daily per man. The only vegetables were a third of a pint of dried peas twice a week but no fruit or lime juice. The cargo was mainly brandy (how galling for the crew!), fabrics (especially finished cottons), linens and woollens, and iron in the form of castings and bars. There was also 'bleaching powder' (chloride of lime) which was thought to be useful in the control of cholera.

8. The *Three Bells*. Lithograph published by Metzler and Co

Other players in the drama were also on the high seas. On or about the 29th of November the *Kilby* had left New Orleans for Boston with a cargo of cotton. The *Napoleon* left Matanzas (Cuba) on December 8th with a cargo of molasses, bound for Portland (Maine), the primary ice-free winter seaport for Canada. The *Maria* and the *Antarctic* were making for Liverpool, the latter from New York.

The scene was gradually developing. The *San Francisco* was fully loaded and most of the passengers were on board by the evening of 21st December. The sea route was risky but it was preferred by the army because disease had previously claimed the lives of many soldiers travelling west via the Isthmus of Panama.

After a delay due to the late arrival of Major George Taylor and his wife, the *San Francisco* finally nosed out of the North Hudson River on the 22nd December. The Major was not pleased with his allocated accommodation, it was 'too far aft'. Lieutenant Lucien Loeser, his wife Sarah and her sister Lucia were reluctant to exchange their airy suite on the saloon deck for much less spacious quarters below, but Major Taylor was the senior officer. Lucia, writing of her experience six months after she returned home, had been reluctant to board the *San Francisco* at all after seeing her being towed back to port[67]. Her father had reassured her that with the condenser removed, the engine 'was perfectly strong and the ship well built.' The first evening Lucia went briefly on deck with a friend and felt sorry for the soldiers quartered there, shivering and stamping their feet to try to get warm. It had snowed the previous night and the youngsters probably felt treated little better than the animals in their nearby pens.

The commanding officer of the Third Regiment, Colonel William Gates, was travelling with his wife and three sons, two of whom had measles. Dr Satterlee, regimental surgeon, had written to the Colonel advising that no child who had, or might be incubating, measles should travel. The doctor believed measles to be more dangerous than smallpox on a ship but the Colonel thought it merely a childish complaint and tore up the letter. At nine o'clock on the first evening, Lucia heard the Colonel say that he was going on deck to make sure his boys were 'comfortably fixed' for the night – she thought he was referring to his children!

For a day or so everything was 'pleasant, people being cheerful and friendly, the sun shining and the sea calm' and at the table 'all was mirth and ease'. Crowded as they were, the men below decks had little fresh air but still 'the jest and laugh went round'. Mr Southworth, a merchant from Rio wrote[68]:

> *The noble vessel glided through the water as if she had long known old ocean... her motion was easy, and the gilt phoenix upon her wheelhouse seemed to extend its golden head and wings to speak its joy for a new triumph in steam navigation.*

On Christmas Eve the wind got up and freshened and many passengers were seasick, including Lucia – 'the steamer pitches dreadfully... I could not sleep and my heart beat quicker at any roll of the ship'. By midnight a tremendous gale had developed. The ship plunged violently through a sea which was a 'mass of foam, boiling and swelling like a cauldron'. Now soaked through and numb with cold, the soldiers on deck – some of whom had been injured – clung to whatever they could find in the darkness. The noise was tremendous: shrieking of the rigging, groaning of the spars, shouts of the crew and the crashing of waves. Animals whose pens had blown away slid chaotically round the deck; some were washed overboard and others were shot. Having crawled to a hatch to look outside, Dr Wirtz (assistant surgeon) described the still moments when the ship crested a huge wave before sliding down into the terrifying trough. At 1.15 am the air-exhaust pump failed and the engines stopped. All the sails had been torn to ribbons in spite of efforts to reef them. Now without power, the *San Francisco* was completely at the mercy of the elements.

At 7 am on Christmas Day the foremast snapped with a tremendous crash and went overboard with its spars, rigging and half the lifeboats. Colonel Burke ordered as many soldiers as possible to get inside the upper saloon. They stood packed shoulder to shoulder in their wet clothes, some crying with cold and fear.

Two hours later a huge wave swept over the ship, taking with it most of the promenade deck, everyone and more or less everything on the main deck, the saloon superstructure with all those inside, one of the paddle guards, the smokestacks and the remaining lifeboats, spare sails and animals. Some people were killed and many injured by flying debris, but the majority drowned. Captain Gardiner got below decks after his servant warned him just in time (and died for his action); the man sleeping next to him was killed instantly by a huge splinter of wood that pierced his head.

There were only two survivors of those who were washed overboard – Mr Rankin (a sutler, selling provisions to the army) and Mr Frederick Southworth (a merchant), who described what happened to him:

I found myself rolling like a top in the water, with salt brine rushing into my mouth and nearly blinding me... when I came to the surface again I was half a mile from the steamer... I seized hold of another piece [of timber] and made the best of my way to the steamer. Two or three huge swells soon tossed me near the ship, I grasped a rope forward of the wheelhouse to which I clung for refuge, rising and falling with the pitching vessel. Losing my strength I dropped from the rope to which I clung and fortunately a friendly wave threw me against the guard of the vessel, which I seized hold of and the next plunge carrying me still higher on the guard, I was enabled at last to climb upon the forward deck and there with my hand broke open a state room window into which I crawled, half-drowned.

Mr Southworth was actually blinded by blood pouring from a scalp wound, a discovery he made after he had recovered a little. Survivors described the horror of being completely unable to help those who had been swept overboard, many of whom were bleeding copiously from their injuries. 'The sea was covered with drowning people', the eldest son of Colonel Gates among them. About 140 people died[69], including Major Taylor and his wife who were last seen holding hands in the water wearing life-preservers.

Lucia put on a dressing gown and thick skirt over her nightdress but could not find any shoes or stockings in the dark. The Loeser family ran to the saloon but the sea poured down onto them. They fought their way up the stairs to the deck with water coming 'in torrents from above and were completely drenched in a few moments.... A roll of the ship would throw us off our footing and all would fall together.'

The *San Francisco's* first officer, Edward Mellus 'than whom no braver man lives' attempted to cut away the remaining (mizzen) mast with an axe[70] in a valiant attempt to reduce the load on the hull while increasing her stability. The ship would have rolled slightly less far each time without the weight of the mast, but the task proved beyond one man.

According to Mrs Gates (who had lost her eldest son) 'the camp women were shrieking a great deal, but the ladies were clinging to each other and the little ones, and were calm and speechless'. The women were probably desperately trying to discover if their partners were still alive. Men were quickly detailed to hold blankets and mattresses over the damaged decking, but this was not enough and the water level in the ship rose dangerously fast. Teams worked the hand pumps to exhaustion, received a ship's biscuit and a small tot of whisky, slept and worked again. Thirty years after the event, one of the cooks told a reporter, 'I can't tell you, sir, anything about how it was, and nobody can. You have to go through it yourself before you can understand it'[71]. Even these efforts were not sufficient, so chains of men (a woman who offered was turned away) bailed and passed buckets of water up through the engine rooms. Mr Aspinwall, though sick, worked this way for several hours until completely exhausted. Some army officers worked for two hours and tried to sleep for two hours round the clock, organising the troops in the bailing lines and at the pumps.

Others started to clear the ship of anything that could be dumped, including the now useless coal, 'each man knew he worked for his life, all worked with a will.' Not everyone shared this view. Lucia saw some of the men hiding under mattresses in order to avoid working – but many were young, untrained recruits and they may have simply been terrified. Enormous waves continued to buffet the ship and the storm howled all around them. The chief engineer, John Marshall, worked almost without sleep for fifty hours in his attempts to restart the engines, only taking brief naps lying 'on a grating'.

Through all this, the women and children were huddled in wet blankets, sometimes without light and often thirsty because getting to the fresh water pump was very dangerous – three or four men detailed to fetch supplies were swept overboard. Lucia's family sat on the floor of the galley in several inches of seawater with their arms around each other 'prepared to meet our sad fate... a fearful death. It was useless to think of touching a life preserver as we did not wish to prolong our misery'. Lucien wrapped a soaking blanket round her frozen and injured feet which made her a little more comfortable. Eventually they were taken one at a time to a dry cabin and put into berths in their wet clothes, but 'the place was full of soldiers... the language of the men and their recklessness was truly horrible.' Lucia listened to the officers cajoling men to work and became aware the whisky casks had been broached. Captain Judd put a guard on a few of these and ordered the rest destroyed; they could not risk mass drunkenness.

Such comfort as there was came from Captain Watkins's calm leadership and constant reassurance and to the tireless efforts of Lieutenant Murray, the ship's mates, the Padre and most of the army officers – with the notable exception of Colonel Gates. He stayed in the forward cabin with his wife, remaining children and a few of his officers and their families.

Later that day the brig *Napoleon* was sighted with the Stars and Stripes flying upside down to indicate distress – she was leaking, short on provisions and had lost some sails. Messages were exchanged about the possibility of rescuing a few passengers[72]. The *Napoleon* stood by that night but at dawn the ships had lost sight of each other. Around midday on December 26th the *Napoleon* reappeared and Lieutenant Winder saw her crew collecting some of the provisions thrown overboard for them[73] from the *San Francisco*. He later said he may have been mistaken but the casks were certainly *res derelicta* (things thrown away) and were retrieved by men who were hungry.

The *Napoleon* then put about and sailed out of sight, to the dismay of those on the stricken ship.

Another brig, the *Maria* of Liverpool, came within hailing distance of the *San Francisco* and was spoken with. Captain Freeman said he would stay by the wreck but the next day the *Maria*, too, had disappeared. A 'Lady Passenger' wrote a long letter to the Editor of the *New York Daily Times*, evidently a friend, explaining what it felt like to be abandoned:[74]

> *And when the morning dawned, and eyes, through the cold gray mist, swept the horizon; <u>there was no ship</u>. The silence of that hour was awful. Anguish was mute, despair was mute. There were some, who have asked for forgiveness since, who thought that the good God had deserted us.*

Lucia and her sister were moved back to the saloon which had been hastily repaired to keep the water out, but it was dark and airless. When the engines were restarted briefly on December 27th, the frail partitioning separating the saloon from the engine room fell away and the space was filled with steam. Lucia wrote 'it really seemed to me that we had escaped one fearful death to face one still more fearful', but not one complaint was uttered', though the injured Dr Satterlee begged to be carried outside for some cool air, which was done. The engines broke down again after only ten minutes, allowing those in the saloon to breathe freely but ending any realistic hope that the ship might still be saved. An unfortunate helmsman who had been lashed to the wheel when the engines were restarted was carried below with a broken leg.

On the same day, a sailor called Alexander drowned. The storm was still raging and the ship was being bailed and pumped round the clock. Everyone was permanently wet, cold, hungry and exhausted from work and lack of sleep. There was little hot food because it was usually too dangerous to light the stoves – and mostly there was just cold water to drink. Colonel Gates was still hardly to be seen and gave no orders or words of encouragement and comfort to anyone[75]. In the afternoon of 27th, the bark *Kilby* was sighted. Messages were exchanged and her Captain, Edwin Low, promised to stay nearby. All were very thankful when the *Kilby* was still there the next day, the fifth of the storm. Sailing close to the *San Francisco*, Low reported he had only one barrel of fresh water and was running out of other provisions. The rough weather abated a little and Captain Watkins was rowed over to commission the *Kilby* for the United States Army. It was Captain Low's first command. He was worried that his ship's insurance would be invalidated and asked the older man for advice. Captain Watkins scribbled an agreement in pencil which both signed, Low resolutely refusing any personal reward. It was intended that everyone on the *San Francisco* except some of her crew would be transferred to the *Kilby*. Captain Watkins had not yet given up all hope of somehow preserving what was left of his ship.

Lieutenant Loeser took ten men and rowed over to jettison some of the *Kilby*'s cargo of cotton. At about three in the afternoon a hawser was fixed between the ships and the rescue began. There was considerable concern that the small boats would be swamped with people and the scene was one of great confusion; some of the army officers were wearing their swords. Colonel Gates made a speech hoping that all would follow his example and wait quietly for their names to be called by rank, saying that he would be the last to abandon ship. Somehow, the first or second boat contained him and his family and he left without appointing anyone in charge of the soldiers still on the *San Francisco*.

Other senior officers left too – including both regimental surgeons – and most of the women and children, altogether about a hundred people. Lucia reported that only four of the ladies had hats. She was wearing some clothes donated by her servant, a dress belonging to her sister and 'half a shawl and a summer hat. I had a fine outfit' (!)

Both ships were rolling heavily in the rough sea, which made the transfer extremely dangerous. Each person was wrapped in blankets and lowered to the rowing boat in a rope sling, caught by Lieutenant Murray. Colonel Burke (who had been seriously injured by falling debris) and Major Merchant (who had fallen into the hold) had to be transported in a tub because they were too weak to hold on to the ropes. One of the Merchant children nearly slipped out of the sling but Lieutenant Murray rescued her. While being rowed across, everyone had to bail water out of the boat and then climb a ladder to the *Kilby's* deck, with a sailor following in case they lost their grip. Some were badly bruised from being thrown against the side of the ship, among them Lucia's sister Sarah.

The cabins allocated to the rescued were packed with people, but they were on their way to safety with hot drinks and something to eat. Later that evening Lieutenant Loeser was rowed back to the *San Francisco* and found Captain Watkins and others at supper. He gave Major Wyse a message of love from his wife on the *Kilby* and asked if there was a reply in the same vein – there was. Loeser returned to the rescue ship with two candlesticks and candles, tea, bread, sugar and several shoulders of bacon. While the lifeboat was being hauled up it was smashed against the side of the ship by the waves, which were getting higher again. Lieutenant Murray reassured everyone that the *Kilby* would ride out the storm, though he cannot have been sure of that. She was old, very creaky and on her way to be overhauled.

Overnight the gale worsened. The connecting hawser between the ships snapped and they drifted apart. Unfortunately not nearly enough provisions or water had been transferred to the *Kilby*.

Meanwhile, on board the *San Francisco*, the head waiter died of cholera, though this was concealed from as many people as possible and his death was blamed on overindulgence in potted meats and fruit. The truth would have caused panic had it been known. Dr Buel, the only medical man left on the *San Francisco*, later described the dreadful conditions in the lower forward cabin where the sufferers lay, unable to get up[76]:

We have here then in operation, excessive overcrowding and accumulated filth, without ventilation, bad air, meagre and insufficient diet. Add to these the strong influence of moral causes... shall we look any further?

Cholera is not contagious but acquired by the ingestion of contaminated food or water. Severe diarrhoea and vomiting is frequently followed by death from dehydration or electrolyte imbalance, sometimes in as little as two hours from the onset of symptoms. In 1854, the cause was unknown and there was no cure. Ironically, that was the year Filippo Pacini isolated the cholera bacterium but his work did not become widely known because it conflicted with the 'miasma' theory of disease[77]. That same year there was an epidemic in Soho. Dr John Snow, who had long believed cholera was spread in drinking water, made a map of the victim's houses and the street pumps they had used. He managed to convince the authorities to remove the handle of a suspect pump, but unfortunately the disease was already abating and his theory was not fully accepted until after the epidemic of 1866[78].

All the drugs on the *San Francisco* had been lost or thrown overboard, although none would have been of any benefit and most treatments for cholera were both unpleasant and harmful[79]. Fortunately the disease did not spread throughout the ship, though an average of ten people died every day and, once, a whole family of four. Sergeant Tom McIntyre had gone over to the *Kilby*, expecting his wife and sons to follow but they had not been able to do so and Mrs McIntyre and the younger child succumbed to cholera. Other passengers 'adopted' the three-year-old boy who was eventually reunited with his father.

The gales continued. Only four army officers were left on the *San Francisco* to look after 325 rank and file troops (mostly recruits) and the remaining camp women and children. These were Major Wyse and Lieutenants Chandler, C. S. Winder and W. A. Winder, who was frequently incapacitated by sea sickness. The *San Francisco* now had to be pumped, bailed and made lighter with fewer men. Cooking could still only be done sporadically so that a cup of tea or a roast potato and piece of bacon was a rare treat. Crew and soldiers survived on ship's biscuit, cold water and the occasional tot of spirits from the small supply left. Many lost hope of rescue and became despondent.

At two in the morning of New Year's Eve, the eighth day of the storm, the fourth officer of the *San Francisco* sighted another ship[80]. William Ewing McDougall, a passenger on the *Three Bells*, reported that Captain Crighton went to him saying there was a ship in distress, showing lights and firing guns. The gunfire continued throughout the night. In the morning Robert steered very close to the *San Francisco* but no shouts could be heard above the noise of the storm. First Mate Gibb and four crew members volunteered to man the one boat still left on the *Three Bells*, but the idea was given up because the sea was too high. A message wrapped round a 'wheel nut' was thrown towards the *Three Bells* but hit the side of the ship and fell into the sea. The second try was more successful but Robert was not impressed by what he read: 'I will charter your vessel for the United States Government. Name your terms. F.O Wyse, U.S Artillery'. He sent a return message that it was essential anyone rescued from the *San Francisco* brought supplies because the *Three Bells* was very low on them. The two ships stayed close to each other for the rest of that day and the following night[81].

Various further messages were exchanged, including 'Be of good cheer, we will not desert you', chalked on pieces of board held up by members of Robert's crew. The *Three Bells* passed quite close to

9. The *San Francisco* Tragedy.
Lithograph by N. Currer, painted by T. Butterworth, 1854

the *San Francisco* several times which required very skilful handling.
Another message said that the *Three Bells* was making four inches
of water an hour and fresh water was very limited but they would
go down rather than abandon the survivors on the stricken ship.
Robert got his crew to line up and cheer at intervals to encourage
those on the *San Francisco*, who cheered back. It was reported that
he had tears in his eyes because he could do no more.

On January 2nd, Captain Watkins supervised the construction of two
rafts and one was launched and tied to the ship. The next day it had gone.

On the eleventh day of the storm, another ship was seen by the
look-out on the *Three Bells* and Robert ordered a distress signal – the
Union Flag flown upside down – to attract her attention[82]. This new
ship, the *Antarctic*, made contact but then the gale freshened and
she sailed about three miles away for safety. On her return the next
morning, January 4th, the weather was much calmer and at last it was

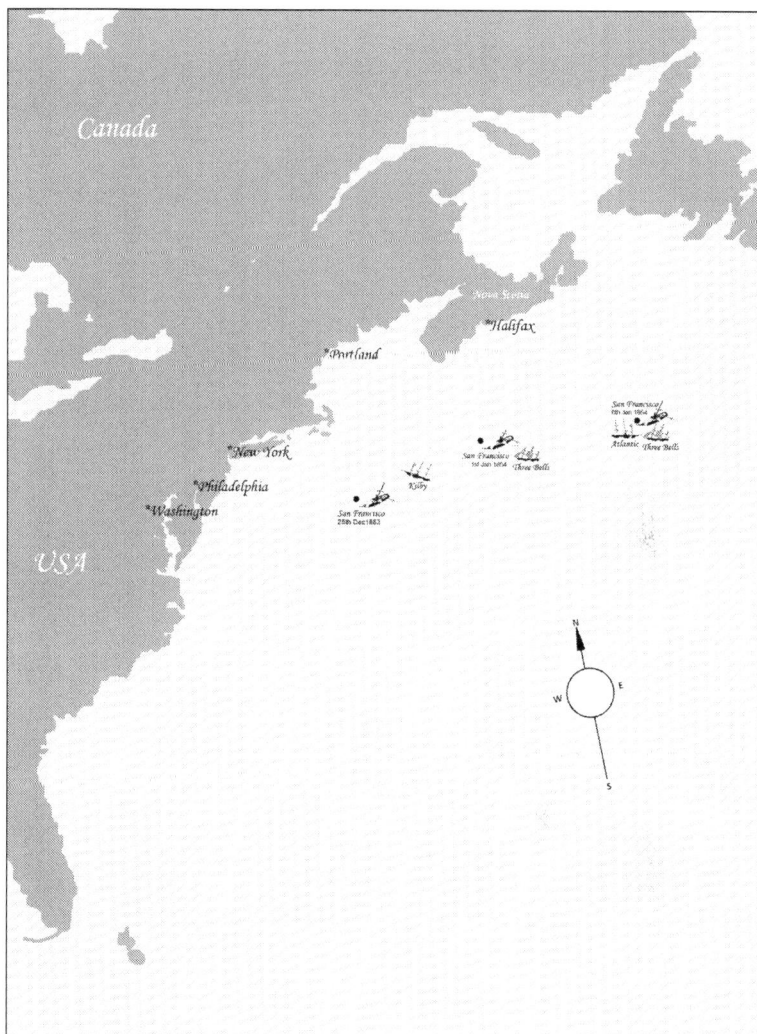

10. Map of the *San Francisco* tragedy. The ships are shown at known co-ordinates, except the *Kilby*, whose position when she left the area of the wreck has been estimated. Drawn by Alan Boyd

safe enough for the rescue to begin. By nightfall seventy to eighty people had been ferried across to safety in small rowing boats and some supplies taken to the *Three Bells*. Guns were fired all night to ensure the ships did not lose each other.

Most of the survivors had been taken off the wreck by the evening of January 5th. Fifteen people transferred to the *Three Bells* were suffering from cholera and a man died while waiting on deck. Some of the ship's officers and crew stayed on the *San Francisco* for a last night, eating ship's biscuit, smoking cigars and apparently sleeping well. Next morning, two weeks after the storm began, they rowed across to the *Three Bells* towing water casks and supplies tied in blankets. A cook, Amos Burgess, described what it all felt like[83]:

We had been ten or eleven days hard at work, expecting death at any minute, fighting the most terrible storm I ever experienced, and for four or five days looking at and admiring the most heroic and complete exhibition of seamanship I have ever seen.

In traditional manner Captain Watkins was the last to leave the *San Francisco*, lowering himself from the bowsprit with the ship's flags wrapped round his waist. He was given nine cheers as he was rowed past the *Three Bells* and boarded the *Antarctic* which then sailed for Liverpool. Finally, the *San Francisco* was scuttled to avoid any danger to other ships[84]. Some were sad to see her abandoned, 'she had been our prison house for fourteen anxious, agonising days and nights. She was near being our grave, yet she was a gallant ship'. The *Three Bells* set sail for New York.

Newspapers reported the loss of many other ships in the same storm; a tragic example:

December 30th 1853. Barque Elizabeth, Strout [the captain] for Matanzas via Holmes Hole for Boston went ashore on the night of Wednesday at Yarmouth. The captain went ashore with his wife in the morning but she died in his arms on the beach – their child which was lashed in the rigging when the vessel struck froze to death.

The *Elizabeth* was later reported as a total loss with all her cargo; only four of the crew were saved[85]. Interestingly, the Captain of the *Napoleon* was also called Strout and had come from Matanzas; perhaps the two men were related.

The wreck of the *San Francisco* was very soon followed by another with an even greater loss of life[86]. During her maiden voyage from Liverpool to Australia, January 21st 1854, the iron clipper RMS *Tayleur* went aground on the east coast of Ireland. Fewer than three hundred of the 660 passengers and crew survived. It was later found that the ship's compasses had not been adjusted for the magnetic field of iron, her rudder was too small and the rope used for the rigging had not been properly stretched. Possibly worse than this, few of the crew were experienced sailors, the rest being 'half-good-for-nothing Lascars, Chinamen and nondescript foreigners' who were not only untrained but could speak little English. The root causes of this disaster were the same as those that sent the *San Francisco* to her doom – impatience, greed and ignorance.

It was extremely bad luck that the *San Francisco* ran into a truly epic storm but her engines had never functioned properly and she was considerably overloaded. More and more ships were lost throughout the Nineteenth Century due to overloading, until a British Member of Parliament, Samuel Plimsoll, began to campaign for a Load Line to be painted on the sides of all ships. This was first done in 1876 but full international agreement concerning Load Lines was not reached until 1930. It seems such a simple and sensible idea, yet it was more than fifty years before it was properly implemented.

Chapter Five

On Board the Rescue Ships

The *Three Bells* was not in particularly good shape herself. Sea water had reacted with the chloride of lime in the hold, causing the release of choking chlorine gas. This pervaded the ship, irritating lungs and causing constant coughing for days, even after all the offending substance had been thrown overboard. Much of the rest of the cargo had also been ditched, including the iron bars. Only one mainsail and one foresail had survived the gales and the ship had sprung a leak which seemed impossible to locate. Water had been pumped out continuously while the *Three Bells* was standing by the *San Francisco*, the crew's efforts augmented by those of the passengers. Luckily engineers were among the rescued and they found and fixed the leak within half an hour. A pipe that supplied water for cleaning the deck had been broken by shifting cargo and some metal had to be cut away before the end could be sealed.

New York was about six hundred miles away when the *Three Bells* left the *San Francisco* on January 6th. At first her progress was slowed by a stiff north-easterly. Fresh water and food were strictly rationed in spite of the additional supplies – just half a pint of water and one ship's biscuit a day was reported. Robert had taken on board all those suffering from cholera and ten of them died during the first night. Fortunately, the sickness 'began to abate almost immediately' and none of the original passengers or crew of the *Three Bells* contracted it. This was attributed to the lingering effects of the chloride of lime, or alternatively to 'moral causes', whatever they may be.

On January 11th the wind turned favourably and the next day they were 'off soundings', *i.e.* offshore in water deeper than a hundred fathoms. No further progress was made that night because 'it grew thick' (fog) but on Friday 13th Robert signalled for a pilot and then a steam tug and, by five in the afternoon, had anchored at New York. This was the first news of the wrecked steamer since the *Napoleon* docked six days before. Newspapers had reported 'the probable loss' of the *San Francisco* with 'eight hundred souls, all of whom are supposed to have perished'[87]. Some pointed out that she was strongly built and might have survived, but each long day made this less likely. Ships were sent to look for the wreck but none found her. It is not difficult to imagine the agonising wait for news, followed by relief for some families as each rescue ship reached safety and the gradual realisation of the rest that there was no hope left.

Many years later, after Robert's death, there was a newspaper article about the rescue and life aboard the *Three Bells* at that time[88]. The reporter had tracked down the chief cook on the *San Francisco*, Amos Burgess, who described the *Three Bells* as 'nice and trim and clean-like, and she was handled so well'. He had little time for the *Antarctic*, 'large, clumsy and didn't handle well'. Amos was among the few who stayed an extra night aboard the doomed ship before being rowed across to the *Three Bells*, which was 'sailing like a peacock'!

Amos described how he took over the galley because the usual cook on the *Three Bells* was confined for intemperance (this man died soon after landing in New York, apparently from exhaustion). He could not speak too highly of Robert, whom he described as 'the most gentle, dignified and courteous man I ever met on board ship. I have never seen, before or since, a sailor who handled his men and his ship with such perfect discipline and correctness.'[89]

Some of those rescued took the opportunity to steal watches and jewellery while on the *Three Bells*. Waiters, cooks and a porter from the *San Francisco* were later tried for the thefts. They had also helped themselves to the possessions of those swept overboard.

On January 16th it was reported that:

Many of the soldiers brought to this port by the Three Bells are
prevented from going on shore for want of apparel.
Major Wyse and command are worn out – they have lost
everything; their six months' pay and supplies and are now
destitute. They will go to Fort Wood tomorrow morning.

Fort Wood was a large battery on Bedloe's Island in the Hudson River, now called Liberty Island, on which stands the iconic statue. The next day's report described how the troops were 'much exhausted by privation and sickness, [but] they appear to be quite comfortable and in good spirits in their quarters.'

Estimates of the number of people rescued on the *Three Bells* vary considerably and reach eight hundred and fifty – more than were actually on board the *San Francisco*. Robert wrote 230 in the ship's log (later lost, but quoted in the press); the number landed in America was 185. Thirty-one adults and six children died and one man jumped overboard, making 223 originally rescued rather than the 230 Robert recorded. The main cause of the deaths on the *Three Bells* was probably cholera, although Caroline Livingstone (a stewardess) – for whom it was a third shipwreck – said that the symptoms were very different from that disease, which she had seen before[90]. 185 is still a large number of people. Assuming an average of two children per survivor and per person down six generations since 1854, there could today be over ten thousand people who owe their existence to Robert Crighton.

The *Antarctic* had left New York for Liverpool without the full complement of passengers for which she was provisioned. When the rescue was underway, Captain Stouffer ordered sufficient berths made up and directed the cooks to make a fresh quarter of beef into soup. About two hundred men, mostly US troops with just two lieutenants to look after them, and nineteen camp women and children were welcomed on board. Hot food and a dry bed must have seemed almost as miraculous as the fact that they were (nearly) safe. No-one on board developed cholera.

Captain Watkins, whose health was reported to be 'seriously impaired' by his ordeal[91], chose to go on the *Antarctic* because he felt he could not abandon all these people to the care of strangers in England. When they reached Liverpool on January 23rd, some of those rescued went to the Waterloo Hotel but the soldiers, women and children remained on board the *Antarctic* anchored in the River Mersey. The American Secretary of War had written to Captain Watkins, asking him to make provision for the comfort of the army officers and soldiers and to make any arrangements he saw fit to return them promptly to the United States.

Lieutenant Charles Winder visited the American consul in Liverpool, Nathaniel Hawthorne (better known for his literary work), to ask for his help but was rebuffed[92]. Hawthorne said he could only aid distressed sailors, not soldiers, and held that officers were responsible for their men even if they were thereby out of pocket. Mr Hawthorne felt he did not have the authority to charter a ship and the agent of the Collins Line ship *Pacific* refused to carry the survivors because all the berths had been sold.

After resting for only a few hours, Captain Watkins took the train to London to request the help of the American Ambassador, James Buchanan, with the repatriation. The *London Standard* commented that the Captain's 'exertions for (the men's) comfort since their arrival in this country have been most praiseworthy.' Watkins probably told the Ambassador about the unhelpful attitude of the Collins Line's agent, because when Buchanan became President in 1857 the US Mail contract with the Line was not renewed, leading to its eventual bankruptcy[93].

By contrast, Charles McIver of the Cunard Line offered the steamship *America* to carry the survivors from Liverpool to Boston. Lieutenant Winder boldly signed the contract for £6,500 and for his leadership was promoted the next year. At only twenty-five he was then the youngest captain in the United States Army. The *America* left England on January 31st and arrived in Boston on February 16th.

All on board were said to be in good health and the troops went on to Newport, Rhode Island. Captain Watkins had a dinner to attend in Boston before giving evidence at the inquiry into the loss of the *San Francisco*, held in New York.

A letter to Captain Stouffer was published on the front page of the *Liverpool Mercury*[94]:

Dear Sir

We, the undersigned passengers on board the American ship Antarctic from the wreck of the steamship San Francisco beg to offer you our sincere gratitude, as a high appreciation of your energy and promptness in rescuing ourselves and commander from the wreck on the 3rd and 4th inst – for your frank, hospitable and warm reception and your uniformly kind hospitality whilst on the voyage. The most whole and generous feelings with which man is endowed could alone have urged such energy and anxiety to rescue us at such a time and under such circumstances. The same has ever influenced you in your treatment of us – in your total disregard for your own comfort and sacrifices for ours.

For your exertions, and those of your officers, in adding to the comfort of our men, women and children, we beg you will accept our deep gratitude, as an humble though sincere tribute of respect for your manly and generous character and high sense of skill as an able commander.

Wishing you health, happiness and success through life we remain, dear Sir, with sincere regard, truly your friends

Jas T. Watkins
Thos L. Schell
Wm G. Rankin (officers of the San Francisco)
C.S. Winder
J.G. Chandler (lieutenants in the Third Regiment)

Life on board the *Kilby* was very different. Lucia Eaton, her sister Sarah and brother-in-law Lieutenant Loeser were rowed over from the *San Francisco* together[95]. The first thing the ladies did was to have a cup of tea, which Lucia described as 'quite refreshing'! The family shared a small cabin – about ten feet by twelve – with twenty-eight other people and more sat in the doorway. The atmosphere was suffocating and the only light came from candles brought by Lieutenant Loeser and stuck on a barrel of 'hard bread' (ship's biscuit) that took up valuable space. Off the cabin were four much smaller areas, each with a berth but no mattress, where a person could 'just turn round'. Eleven people occupied these small rooms, including Colonel Gates and his family (he found a mattress) and Mrs Marshall, wife of the Chief Engineer who had stayed on the *San Francisco*, with her three children.

The first night another terrific storm battered the *Kilby,* making sleep very difficult. The Episcopal Minister, who had been on his way to Brazil as a missionary, asked everyone to read a chapter of the Bible aloud and some ladies sang a hymn. During the long hours of darkness the hawser between the ships snapped and by dawn the *San Francisco* had disappeared. There was a discussion about the best course of action – to look for her or make for port and send assistance. Colonel Gates (naturally, being worried only about himself and his family) and Captain Low, concerned about the state of the supplies – especially water – wanted to sail straight for port. The majority of officers (and the ladies, though they were not, of course, present at the meeting) did not want to abandon so many people to their fate.

It was decided to stand by for a while but there was no sight of the *San Francisco*. The search was abandoned after two days and Captain Low set sail for New York. The lack of provisions meant that everyone was limited to two meals a day – breakfast and tea – for each of which the ration was a ship's biscuit and a slice of bacon. Unfortunately, the *Kilby*'s few remaining sails were old and torn and had to be reefed as soon as the wind freshened and, for a week, any progress they made was immediately lost. After ten days of this ordeal, there was great excitement when a ship was sighted. The crew hoisted a flag upside down to signal distress and set alight a torch made of oakum, cotton and rope covered in tar but both flag and torch were ignored.

Water was now limited to half a pint a person a day with one biscuit and two very small squares of bacon. Lucia commented on how hard it was to hear the children crying for water that could not be given to them, even those feverish with measles. Colonel Gates was heard to say that he would rather twenty men died than one of his children went thirsty. The three mothers who were breast feeding must have been particularly dehydrated themselves and worried that their babies were not getting enough nourishment.

By day twelve, the ration was reduced to half a biscuit, the squares of bacon and very little water. Captain Low found a half barrel of molasses but this made people both sick and thirsty – except for Mrs Gates who 'feasted on' molasses and biscuit[96] Almost everyone had to try to sleep either sitting up or lying on the hard floor, rolled about by waves. Luckily there was a shower of rain, which was collected enthusiastically.

Some of the remaining cargo was corn, which they pounded into a rough flour to make a kind of 'cake' and a mush. But these took too much water (Lucia is a bit confused here because she says sea water was used for its salt content and there was certainly no shortage of that), so the corn was roasted. Colonel Gates was later accused of getting soldiers to grind corn for just his family but, for once, we should perhaps excuse him. Lieutenant Loeser paid a man to do the same for himself, Sarah and Lucia and there was very little else for the men to do.

That day another ship passed without seeing them because no signals could be made in time. On January 11th there was a rainstorm and Lucia mentions snow and the luxury of being able to wash her face and hands in fresh water. She does not say so but, because no-one had a change of clothes or could wash properly, the smell in the overcrowded cabins must have been appalling.

Land was so tantalizingly close on the fifteenth day that the angry and hungry crew almost mutinied, threatening to run the *Kilby* straight onto the shore. Horrified, Lieutenant Murray explained to them that this would kill everyone on board. Eventually the men agreed to wait until the next day before taking this action, though they were determined to do so then.

Luckily and just in time another ship was sighted in the morning, sixteen days after the survivors had left the *San Francisco*. Captain Pendleton of the *Lucy Thompson* from Liverpool overslept for the first time in his life that day, causing some delay, or he would not have come upon the *Kilby*. The *Lucy Thompson* was carrying emigrants but no cabin passengers and Pendleton agreed to take on board everyone who wanted to go. Some civilians and soldiers volunteered to stay behind to help sail the *Kilby* if her crew carried out their threat and mutinied. The transfer was difficult because each person had to climb a ladder in very rough seas, held by a rope under the arms. 'Our blankets were half on us, our hats hanging off, and hair getting loose hanging in wild disorder' (Lucia). History repeated itself when a baby almost slipped out of the sling fashioned to get him/her into the *Lucy Thompson*. Meanwhile, water, provisions and a topgallant sail were sent over to the *Kilby* and Captain Pendleton also promised to send a tug to tow her.

Once aboard the *Lucy Thompson*, the survivors were immediately given some port and bread, which Lucia had once believed she would never see again. There was a final storm that night and she could not sleep much, but breakfast was hot rolls, salt mackerel and biscuits, tea and water. Such luxury. From a passing ship they obtained newspapers and learned that all those left on the *San Francisco* had also been rescued and that some of them were already at New York. This was good news for all, but especially for the families divided between the ships. Mr Aspinwall sent out a tug, the *Titan*, with blankets and warm clothes. The soldiers stayed on the *Lucy Thompson;* the rest boarded the *Titan* which arrived at New York the next day, January 15th, twenty-four days after the *San Francisco* had left.

With what thankfulness must the survivors have stumbled out of the tug onto dry land? They had not been able to change their clothes for seventeen days and had brought nothing else from the sinking ship (except the stolen jewellery). Some stories grow in the telling. When the *Lucy Thompson* arrived at New York on 14th January, the rescued soldiers were said to be 'cold, wet, hungry and almost naked' which seems a little exaggerated. Clothes they may have been short of but they were surely not wet or hungry by then.

The *Kilby* continued towards New York and took on a pilot at Fire Island, but another storm blew her helplessly fifty miles east-south-east of Barnegat. There she was found by the steamer *City of New York* and towed to Boston, arriving in the early hours of January 17th. The passengers were taken to Tremont House (a hotel where Davy Crockett and Charles Dickens once slept) for 'every attention' before most left for New York; the soldiers went to a recruiting office for new uniforms. Later that day Captain Low appeared at the Boston Merchant's Exchange where he was heartily cheered.

There were no deaths on the *Kilby*, though some people were very ill. All those suffering from cholera were taken onto the *Three Bells*, an act of considerable compassion that hardly seems to have been noticed. It would be interesting to know what the passengers originally on the *Three Bells* thought of the rescue; considerable additional risks had been taken with their lives, including the threat of cholera.

Robert's heroism was contrasted, perhaps a little unfairly, with the behaviour of the captains of the ships *Napoleon* and *Maria*. One reporter[97] likened them to the priest and the Levite who passed by on the other side, a direct reference to the parable of the Good

Samaritan; a harsh judgement from someone who was probably sitting behind a desk in a warm, dry room with the expectation of a satisfying lunch. The *Maria* (called *Maria Freeman* in the papers) had reached Liverpool on January 4th or 5th, when Captain Freeman telegraphed America with the last known position of the *San Francisco* and, as a result, three merchant ships were quickly chartered to find her, though a certain Mr Vanderbilt refused to allow his ship the *North Star* to be sent because the storm was still raging.

The *Napoleon* reached Boston two days later, on January 7th, when Captain Strout also immediately telegraphed the position and condition of the *San Francisco*, which by then had almost certainly sunk. The *Napoleon* was leaking when she came upon the *San Francisco*, had lost some sails and rigging and rations were down to three biscuits a day. Her crew members said they had seen the great wave sweep the *San Francisco* but could not have done so because they were not there at the time.

Captain Strout was ill, but had asked his mate for an estimate of how many could be taken on board if provisions came with them. The reply was thirty-two men and some officers in the cabin. Next day Strout gave orders to sail away from the *San Francisco*. When questioned by the man at the wheel, he said his ship would be swamped with desperate people – but also that the *San Francisco* looked in better shape than the *Napoleon*. His decision was understandable, though his crew probably wished it had been otherwise when they discovered how the rescuers had become heroes overnight.

Strout's troubles were not over. After his return to Portland (Maine) in February, he was arrested on a charge of 'brutal treatment to one of his crew'[98]. The case was dismissed, but from the evidence it is clear that Strout was a tyrant with a shrivelled heart. He was not alone; over the second half of the Nineteenth Century the clamour in the British and Australian press about 'the cruelties on board American ships' increased[99]. From a report of the Liverpool Society of Friends of Foreigners in distress[100]:

Hundreds of poor men of all nations are annually cast among us in an utterly wretched condition....from the revolting usage they receive on board the American vessels... men have been forced to draw with their teeth iron nails from the deck... and lick dust from the cabin floor.

We cannot believe that the American Government are aware of the habits and practices of the officers of merchant vessels, now so notorious... or they would have supplied some remedy to what has assumed the proportions of a disease.

Cases of brutality continued to be reported right through the Nineteenth Century:

The George Stetson is the latest of American ships to disgrace the American marine by a record of unspeakable brutality to sailors on the high seas[101].

Chapter Six
Aftermath in America

It must have been the most incredible feeling for everyone on board the *Three Bells* when she finally anchored in the North Hudson River on the evening of Friday January 13th. They were alive! The army officers were invited to Astor House (New York's premier hotel) but what happened to others, such as the camp women and children and the passengers from the *Three Bells*, was not recorded.

Robert became a hero overnight, though he remained on board his ship for some time, unaware of the tsunami of gratitude about to engulf him. Once it became known that two other ships had promised aid and then slipped away leaving hundreds to their fate, the newspapers were full of stories about how the *Three Bells*, in spite of leaking furiously, low on provisions and with only two sails, nevertheless stayed by the wreck for days until the gale abated a little. Robert's message, 'Be of good cheer, we will stand by you' really caught the public's imagination. A reporter asked some of those rescued in the *Three Bells* what they thought of her commander[102]. One answered, 'no language is adequate to describe the kind and considerate manner in which (we) were treated'. James Lorimer Graham, one of the civilian passengers said:

> *To Captain Creighton, of the good ship the Three Bells, I feel that every one of us who were rescued by his instrumentality owe a debt of gratitude that can never be repaid. For my part I shall ever love and honour him as a noble specimen of a generous and true-hearted British sailor. He merits and I trust will receive, a rich reward.*

An officer added 'he is a gentleman, God bless him, he *is* a gentleman.'

For the next few weeks Robert was the man whose hand everyone wanted to shake, cheered and clapped enthusiastically wherever he went. Presented with framed resolutions praising his courage and cheques amounting to a fortune, he repeatedly said that he had only done his duty and expected no more than simple thanks. This was also the original view of one leader writer[103]:

The Loss of the San Francisco. A good word must be said for the Captain of the British ship now in this port... he did his duty and no more, but the blessings of those he saved... will not forsake him.

That same day, an impromptu call 'to acknowledge his noble services' was hurriedly organised by the merchants of New York at the Exchange[104]. Robert, however, did not appear. Perhaps he had not had sufficient time or facilities to make himself presentable but, in any case, he had reports to write and a crew to look after.

On the evening of Sunday, January 15th Robert 'was finally induced to accept the hospitalities of Astor House'. This was a splendid hotel, with water closets and hot and cold water on all five floors. Gas was generated on site and used for lighting; in the early days, some unfortunates blew out the gas as they would a candle and were asphyxiated. All this must have seemed amazingly luxurious to Robert. The proprietors of the hotel declined any compensation for their hospitality to the sufferers and rescuers of the *San Francisco*.

We do not know when Robert managed to get a reassuring message to Jane. However, the probable loss of the *San Francisco* was not reported in any British newspaper until January 19th and the *Three Bells* was not mentioned in connection with this until January 24th, so there was time for a telegraph to have reached the ship owner's office in Glasgow before the newspapers got hold of the story.

On 16th January, one of the crew of the *Three Bells* died, it was said from exhaustion. He left a widow and two children and the writer of a letter in the *New York Times* hoped that they would receive some compensation. Another letter, from Elijah R. Brown, was printed in the same paper with the editorial comment that it 'will put public credulity to a test of unusual severity'. Sergeant Brown wrote that he was washed off the *San Francisco* three times and jumped into the sea once to save a picture which had fallen out of his jacket. And $1150 in gold had been stolen from his trunk (!!)

Next day, there was a service of thanksgiving in Grace Church, Brooklyn, to which the survivors were invited, although some mistakenly went to a church of the same name in Broadway. All the army officers (except three or four who were exhausted) attended to keep a vow they had made when facing imminent death. It is not clear if the rank and file soldiers went to the service before going to Bledloe's Island, but a small group of rescued children joined in the singing and prayers. The atmosphere was mournful rather than cheerful. In the afternoon Robert went to the Rotunda of the Merchant's Exchange accompanied by a Mr James Lee. Nine cheers were heartily given and Robert 'bowed politely' in acknowledgement – at which there were even more cheers and much clapping.

Meanwhile, on January 18th Captain Low wrote to Lieutenant Fremont about the alteration to the contract he had made with Captain Watkins[105]. The original had been written in pencil but a council of army officers led by Major Wyse altered it, adding five per cent primage (on the value of the cargo) and a thousand dollars to be paid to Captain Low. As soon as he was aware of these additions, he wrote:

The agreement in ink is not exactly like the one in pencil... I did not work for gain and I want it withdrawn. The primage I got from my owners – I do not want it twice.

Colonel Gates wrote from Astor House that he and the other officers of the Third Regiment of Artillery 'desire to express the high sense they entertain of the gallant conduct and gentlemanly bearing of Captain Watkins' and trusted he would not be forgotten by the noble citizens of New York. The merchants of Philadelphia met to return thanks to the three captains, to ask Congress to act quickly in the matter of the sufferers and rescuers and to start a testimonial fund.

On Friday, January 20th, a letter from a Dr Castle was printed in the *New York Daily Times*. He seemed determined to prove that the disease on board the San Francisco had not been cholera because the cabin passengers had 'free, pure ventilation and no doubt better nourishment... consequently their blood would not have become carbonized[106] in addition to the loss of nervous force'. In spite of this spectacular lack of *evidence-based medicine* (the late Twentieth Century's medical Holy Grail), he concluded that in future ships should practice 'cleanliness in its most comprehensive sense'. In which, of course, he was absolutely correct.

Robert was in demand:

Captain Creighton of the Three Bells. – This heroic officer whose gallant conduct at the wreck of the San Francisco has elicited so much admiration recently visited Brady's gallery and sat for his portrait, which is now on exhibition at no 359 Broadway over Thompson's saloon[107].

This may have been one of the portraits printed on the sheet music dedicated to him; the whereabouts of the original is unknown. At midnight on January 21st Robert attended the Thistle Ball at Montague Hall in Brooklyn, 'when he was received with every mark of respect'.

The courtesies continued. On January 22nd, this graceful letter was published in the *New York Daily Times*:

R.B.Forbes, Esq Boston.

Dear Sir

I have just received yours of the 20th instant, and now beg to reply to your questions. I expect to leave this City for Glasgow on the 1st proximo.

I enclose a slip of the names of my officers, and those of the crew who are most deserving, and as they will receive complimentary testimonials from the fund subscribed by the New York merchants, it may be of more service to them to receive in money whatever the Boston merchants may seem proper to give. I would also suggest that the money should not be given to any of the seamen until they arrive at Glasgow[108]. As for my proportion, I respectfully decline giving any opinion. The thanks I have received, from so many grateful hearts, have amply repaid me for doing my simple duty, in being the means, through providence, of rescuing so many of my fellow-creatures from their perilous position.

As to the contract with me at the wreck, I received many offers to charter or sell my ship and cargo, but replied we would consider about that when we arrived at New York; and after anchoring off the Battery, Major Wyse requested to have a contract signed, which was done. I have no interest in the ship, and being so long delayed at the wreck, this contract was made to secure my owners and shippers of cargo.

With many thanks for your kind congratulations, I am, dear Sir, yours truly,
ROBERT CRIGHTON

This seems to sum up the nation's feelings towards Robert:

The generous conduct of Captain Creighton touched more hearts than those whose lives he preserved. Speaking as he did, in a voice louder than the tempest, precious words of promise to persons in such appalling danger he has won the grateful admiration of hundreds of thousands he will never meet. He is a native of Port Glasgow, about twenty miles lower down the Clyde than the city of Glasgow and is 32 years of age... He has a wife and child, is 6 feet high, full-chested and broad shouldered and the loss of some of his sails during the storm which wrecked the San Francisco is the worst mishap that ever befell him upon the ocean, though he has been in storms not a few[109].

Robert was made an Honorary Freemason at Holland Lodge, taking his First (Entered Apprentice) and Second (Fellowcraft) degrees. In a published address (1878) by Joseph N. Balestier, these honours were said to be due to the efforts of a Brother Edward Bell and caused 'immense excitement in the Masonic world[110]'.

Not everything was sweetness and light. Mrs Gates had reported looting on the *San Francisco* by waiters, soldiers and camp women[111] and some of the miscreants were not very streetwise about selling the stolen goods. Two crew members visited a jeweller's shop in New York offering a package of jewellery at seventy-five per cent below its true value. They were detained and taken into custody. Some items had once been the property of those who had died on the *San Francisco* and the rest were stolen on the *Three Bells.* Major Wyse had already offered a reward of a thousand dollars for the return of his watch, a wedding present from his wife[112].

Within the hour of their arrest, Robert visited the men in gaol[113]. They confessed immediately afterwards and were locked up to await trial. A porter was later charged with the same offences. Another man, John Logan, tried to sell a set of lancets with tortoiseshell handles belonging to the army surgeon and was also imprisoned. All those arrested were of Afro-Caribbean descent and Mr Logan was most indignant that no white men had been charged. He offered to identify others he knew who had also stolen property from luggage.

In Congress, it was agreed that eight month's pay and rations should be advanced to the surviving soldiers and not charged to them, and that widows and minor children of those who died should be paid the same pension they would have received had their men been killed in battle. Senator Jones moved an amendment that the losses of those on board be ascertained and reimbursed. It had been suggested that this would 'open the door too wide' but he thought benevolence and magnanimity were to be recommended. He mentioned a 'poor fellow, a sergeant, who had saved eight hundred dollars', the whole of which had been swept away leaving him penniless. (Elijah Brown seems to have found one believer, even if he did vary the amount he had supposedly lost.) But at this point Senator Shields referred to reports that some army officers were among the first men to leave the *San Francisco*. It was said that the Colonel and all the officers, including the surgeons, had left their troops 'who did not know where to find either provisions or medical stores'. Shields suggested that this should delay payment. If it was true of the Commander, then he was as guilty of abandoning his post as if he had deserted on the field of battle. Mr Jones then withdrew his amendment[114].

Robert went to the theatre that evening.

On January 25th, some of the jewellery stolen from luggage on board the *San Francisco* was identified in court[115]. An elegant diamond brooch and pearl earrings belonging to Mrs Taylor, the wife of Major George Taylor (both of whom had died) were recognised by their employee, Margaret Parker[116].

That evening there was a Grand Ball at the Metropolitan Hotel, New York:

At half past eleven o'clock the gallant Captain Creighton entered the ball room, leaning upon the arm of E.K.Collins, Esq. He was immediately the observed of all observers and every attention was paid to him that gratitude and admiration could suggest on the part of the company. The heroic Captain appeared to enjoy himself and during the evening frequently expressed his delight at the dazzling brilliance around him.

Supper was from 11 pm to 2 am and they danced till dawn[117]. Next day, Robert was presented with the Freedom of the City of New York. Alderman Blunt made the presentation[118]:

Captain Robert Crighton – Sir, I am authorised by the Corporation of the city of New York to extend to you the freedom of this city, together with a gold box, as a testimonial of their regard for you. I might linger on the thrilling incidents connected to your fidelity to suffering humanity. From the moment you discovered the San Francisco until you had rescued from a watery grave more than 200 distracted beings, I might touchingly allude to your tears from day to day, as witnessed by your sailors, because you could not sooner relieve the unfortunate. I might speak of the fearful responsibility you assumed in violating the insurance of your ship and valuable cargo, by deviating from your specific course – of your personal perils amid the howling tempest – of the four-inch stream of water pouring in upon you, which compelled both pumps to be constantly wrought before you discovered the wreck – of the disadvantages of 400 tons of iron, and large quantities of merchandise in a ship of only 700 tons burthen – of the loss of every sail before you saw the wreck, save your foresail and mainsail – I might dwell on these historical truths, and on your affectionate regard for the rescued, but I forbear. All this, and even more, is on every tongue and uttered around every fireside, and cannot be glorified by me. The contemplation of the good you have affected will ever be a delightful solace to you, and your humanity will be a precious inheritance for your consanguity; the wives and children of those whose lives you preserved will ever love you, and transmit your name to their furthest posterity; the mariners of every ocean will strive to imitate your meritorious example; the noble youth of our country will read of your heroic deeds, and resolve

*to cultivate your manly virtues; little children already lisp your name
in terms of praise; tears of gratitude are freely shed for you by both
sexes; and fervent prayers go up to heaven from all the habitations
of this land, that your valuable life may long be preserved, and that
health, happiness and prosperity may ever be your lot; and your
name will be revered by coming generations, when every being who
beholds this day's sun shall be a tenant of the tomb.*

Along with the 'usual forms of the freedom of the city', Robert
was presented with a gold snuff box. He was 'much overcome' and
thanked the Committee, repeating that he had only done his duty.

They then went by carriage to the Governor's Room at City
Hall where many citizens were waiting to meet Robert. General
Winfield Scott, veteran of the Mexican-American War and called
the 'greatest living general' by the Duke of Wellington, said he was
glad to shake such a noble man by the hand and thanked him for his
kindness to the men he (Scott) commanded. One 'fine-looking old
gentleman' said he would rather take the captain's hand than that of
the proudest monarch who ever sat upon a throne. In a nice touch,
a little apprentice boy entered the room with his shirt sleeves rolled
up to his shoulders and on meeting Robert said, 'Be of good cheer'.
Upwards of two thousand people including several ladies, one of
whom 'rapturously kissed his hand', met their hero that day.

Afterwards Robert and the Committee went to Astor House,
where he was presented with a framed copy of the preamble and
resolutions passed by the boards of the Common Council. At the
top were the American and 'English' (British, perhaps) flags and,
under them, a picture of the *Three Bells* rescuing people from the
wrecked steamer, the whole in a handsome gilt frame.

There was then a private dinner at Astor House and in the
evening 'the gallant captain' saw 'Uncle Tom's Cabin' on Broadway,
in a private box draped with the American and English (again!) flags.

11. Gold Snuff Box from the City of New York

Despite the unpleasant weather, there were many beautifully dressed ladies in the audience who had come to see 'the brave and intrepid rescuer of so many'. Robert was greeted with such enthusiasm that the walls of the theatre were said to tremble. He responded 'with a bashful bow' and the band played 'Scots wae ha'e wi Wallace bled' (*Scots which have with Wallace bled*), then the unofficial Scottish National Anthem. Composed by Robert Burns from a speech made by Robert the Bruce before Bannockburn when the ill-prepared Scots army faced a much larger English one, it is about not giving up in the face of adversity and is still sung at the annual conference of the Scottish National Party.

The dinner and snuff box together cost $348.25 and later there was some scandal because no record of payment for these could be found in the City's accounts. Alderman Blunt admitted to footing the bill himself because he was worried that otherwise the occasion might not be sufficiently splendid.

On January 28th it was reported that the *Three Bells* 'has been crowded with visitors anxious to see the vessel and the commander'.

Three days later Robert took the third degree of Masonry, that of Master. It is not known if he ever attended any meetings afterwards, but he was in good standing when he died.

Robert and Edwin Low travelled to Philadelphia on February 1st, where a suite of rooms had been reserved for them at the splendid Girard House Hotel. Next day they were welcomed almost too enthusiastically, as recorded by Mark Twain[119]:

I went with a few friends, to the Exchange, to see the reception of the two lions, Captains Low and Crighton. The Reading Room, at 12 o'clock, was densely crowded. About five minutes past twelve the two heroes made their appearance, and were received with three times three by the assembled populace. After a few remarks by the President of the testimonials committee, the shaking of hands commenced, and the two Captains were borne through the crowd, to the great danger of their lives and limbs, and were thus squeezed and cheered into the street, where a carriage was in waiting to convey them to the State House. The crowd followed them on the run, yelling and huzzaing till they were out of sight. The money subscribed for each, I believe, was about $2,500, in addition to which they are to receive several medals.

There was a suggestion in the newspapers that Robert might be presented with a ship[120], sometimes even named as the *Rescue*, but it was only a rumour.

In the morning the two captains were shown the attractions of Philadelphia and afterwards met the merchants at the Exchange. They were handed the resolutions of their committee, 'handsomely engrossed', and the cheques, which they received with a modest bow. The resolutions were read aloud and included:

'Captains Crighton and Low are entitled to the grateful thanks of the civilized world. In no quarter of the globe can the generous actions of these distinguished seamen be more highly or justly appreciated than by this community. We extend to these Good Samaritans the right hand of friendship.'

The speaker went on to say that Captain Crighton's name had been incorrectly spelled (presumably on the resolution and cheque). He thought that this should be put right because his name was destined to be enrolled in the Temple of Fame. Laughter and cheers greeted this suggestion.

Robert then got up on a chair and was warmly greeted. He said he found it impossible to express the feelings of his heart after the kindness with which he had been received, and simply added 'I am much obliged to you'. Edwin Low also expressed his thanks and then there was a great surge to shake the captains by the hand. It seemed prudent for them to leave but it was a struggle to get to the waiting carriage and people climbed onto it, still wanting to shake hands.

The two men were driven to the Hall of Independence and had a panoramic view of the city from its steeple. Back at ground level and standing near the statue of George Washington, the Mayor addressed them with even more hyperbole than the Chairman of the Merchant's Committee[121]:

It does not happen to many, in your way of life, to witness what you saw so recently on the deep sea. I regret that it is the good fortune of fewer still to be able to act as you have acted amid scenes which truly 'tried men's souls'. The mariner who from his own quarter deck saw hundreds of his fellow men in a tempest-tossed, disabled and sinking craft and as he hailed her gave utterance to the sentiment 'Be of good cheer, I will not desert you' earns and deserves an immortality of

fame. 'I will not desert you'. What anguish did those words and that
promise allay – how soothing to the desolate and broken-hearted!
Still less, if less at all, in praise and reward is due to him who, with
a craft disabled and almost a wreck, came to the rescue of his fellow
man in greater peril and extremity.

After both Captains had briefly thanked the Mayor, many more
people lined up to shake their hands – which must have been bruised
by this time – until they were escorted to the 'New York cars' (train
carriages). Readers were told that 'Captain Crighton is a Scotchman,
in height over six feet and Captain Low is an American.' One reporter
asked Robert what he thought of the people of Philadelphia. He replied
with much emotion that he could never forget them and repeated yet
again that he had only ever expected the thanks of those he had rescued.

By the end of the first week in February, the money collected to
reward the captains and crews of the *Three Bells*, the *Kilby* and the
Antarctic was over eighty-four thousand dollars[122]. It was also expected
that 'something handsome will be done by the National Legislature
at Washington which is always tardy in its movements'. This turned
out to be a very accurate observation; it was twelve years before the
enabling legislation was passed.

Robert was still getting some press attention:

Captain Creighton expects to leave for Europe (soon)... He is
continually receiving letters of congratulation and thanks from all
parts of the Union and would allow them to be published were it not
that he fears it would have a tendency to give him an unwished for
notoriety. He will carry out a cargo of breadstuffs, besides a number
of passengers who have already made application for passage[123].

Somewhat ironically, on February 13th Robert was the guest of
honour at an entertainment on board the *Pacific* at New York[124]. This

was the very ship of the Collins Line whose captain had declined to take home those rescued in the *Antarctic*.

By February 17th, one newspaper reporter must have been short of new things to say about Robert, who would have been surprised to learn that he had 'determined to become a citizen of the United States and either has, or is about to, declare his intentions to that effect'. There was no follow-up to this piece of creative writing[125].

When the *Three Bells* was cleared from the port of New York preparatory to sailing for home, several newspapers published a farewell and best wishes to Robert, including that he might never need 'succour from others'. The reporter had 'no doubt that (Captain Creighton) will receive from his own countrymen that testimonial for his brave and persevering conduct' – he could hardly have been more wrong.

Just two months after Robert left America, Captain Corish of the *Mohongo* rescued the crew of the crippled *Argo*, even though his ship was 'considerably damaged' by the same gale that had turned the *Argo* onto her beam ends. His bravery merited only brief reports in the papers, prompting one reporter to wonder where all the testimonials were on this occasion and if they 'must all heaped on one hero?' This seems a fair, if slightly sour, comment[126].

Finally, in April 1866 the Bill providing for medals and $7,500 to be awarded to the captains of the *Three Bells*, the *Kilby* and the *Antarctic* 'as testimonials of national gratitude for their gallant conduct in rescuing about 500 Americans from the wreck of the steamship *San Francisco*' was passed in the US Senate. Financial rewards were also to be made to the officers and crews of these ships. It would be interesting to know how it was thought possible to trace these people after such a long time (sailors changed ships frequently, went all over the world, sometimes used pseudonyms and occasionally deserted) and how successful the search was.

Chapter Seven

The *Tornado* Years

Robert was ill for a few days in February[127] but by the middle of the month was at last ready to leave New York. The *Three Bells* was cleared out of the harbour on February 14th 1854 and left for Glasgow on 20th. A journalist described the scene[128]:

> *The anchor being weighed, the Three Bells stood down the bay in tow of the steamer Jacob Bell. As the ship passed Governor's Island a salute of thirty-one guns was fired from the fort, after which Major Sprague gathered the soldiers upon the ramparts and saluted Captain Creighton with more rounds of stentorian cheers than we could count. The cheers were no less heartily returned by the crew and guests on the Three Bells, and the Union Jack and Stars and Stripes dipped gracefully to each other. Passing Bedloe's Island, another salute of thirty-one guns was fired from that fort, after which the soldiers, many of whom had cause to remember the brave Captain with gratitude, cheered him heartily....as the Three Bells passed the different craft in the river she was saluted with steam whistles, bells and cheers. Subsequently a handsome entertainment was prepared on board the Three Bells, and Capt. Creighton parted with his friends with the kindest wishes on both sides.*

The cargo was largely food items: lard, beef, flour, butter, bacon, oil of peppermint, cornmeal and apples. There was also whale oil, tallow, staves, leather and spirits of turpentine in barrels[129]. Being a fire hazard, turpentine was not usually carried in the hold and, on this voyage, the barrels were lashed to the bulwarks slightly above deck level. The main use of turpentine was medicinal and it is still a component of Vicks Vapour rub. Captains were generally allowed to carry some cargo on their own account and two barrels of flour were listed as belonging to Robert.

Astonishingly, or at least unluckily, very bad weather continued to track the *Three Bells*. There were small paragraphs in several newspapers reporting that she had got to Glasgow in sixteen days, a record for a sailing ship although she actually arrived on March 11th, which is nineteen days. During the voyage she had met gale after gale and 'several tremendous seas struck her' almost destroying the captain's cabin[130]. Robert lost clothes, charts and some of 'the presents he had been given' in America. The log book was washed overboard along with many of the crew's personal possessions. They had no dry clothes for days. When the ship no longer responded to the helm because of the weight of water on board, Robert ordered that the casks of turpentine be emptied. A passenger reported that 'the Captain scarcely expected to be obeyed as all hopes of being saved had well-nigh been given up' although this seems unlikely. Robert's crews respected him and they would have known that lightening the ship was the only way to save her – and themselves. As the turpentine drained away, the *Three Bells* rose in the water and the cabin could be pumped out, after which she could be steered again. One unfortunate man fell from the rigging during the storm and was drowned.

No cheers (apparently) greeted the *Three Bells* on her return to Glasgow. She was simply recorded as having arrived, although in February there had been some brief references to Robert's heroism in the British newspapers including details of the money collected for him and the likelihood of his being given a ship. The *Glasgow Herald* reprinted a passenger's account of the wreck of the *San Francisco* from the New York papers[131] and also published this paean under 'Town Council Proceedings' the day before the *Three Bells* returned[132]:

The New York papers in noticing the departure of the Three Bells for the Clyde on the 21ˢᵗ February speak as follows-

Homeward Bound. *A salute of twenty-one guns was fired from old Fort Columbus, Governor's Island, at eleven o'clock this morning. The roar of cannon, on this occasion, is no 'earthquake voice of victory' proclaiming a triumph of men over men. It heralds the approach of no bloodstained conqueror. It speaks not of battle nor of blood. It is not in honor of the arrival of some laurelled hero, nor of the departure of what the world is in the habit of calling 'great men'. No. Gunpowder for once merely tells of a farewell a grateful people are taking of a plain and unpretending British sailor – not bidding him such a farewell because he is plain and unpretending but because he has shown that he has within him that which a Napoleon, a Caesar or an Alexander never had – a big heart, and a bravery in the cause of humanity which scorns all self and stimulates the possessor of it to deeds of heroism of a more ennobling kind than any that is born and brought up on the field of battle. God speed the Three Bells on her homeward voyage. Health and long life to the gallant Crighton! Fair be the breezes that waft them back from the Hudson to the Clyde. A British flag, it is true, floats at the peak; but for all time to come the Three Bells is essentially an American ship. Her name is already a household word among us, to be lisped when wintry winds, and storms, and tempests revive, at the hearthstone, the melancholy memories of the awful occasion which showed the world how ignorant it was till then of one of its really greatest men.*

And that was that, the councillors did not discuss making Robert a freeman of the city of Glasgow or even whether to hold a civic reception.

It seems that the money collected for Robert in America and forwarded to the ship's owners may have been appropriated by them (see Appendix 1). If true, this was bare-faced theft because the United States Government had already paid generous compensation ($25,000) for the loss of cargo and the extra time the ship had been away. Two of the *Three Bells'* owners were brothers, William and Finlay Bell, the third was their cousin John Bell[133]. Both John's butchery business in Argyll Street, Glasgow and the building of the *Three Bells* may have been financed by Archibald Fullarton, a wealthy businessman who was probably related to them. (One of John's daughters was called Harriet Fullarton Bell.) Two of the Bells lost a great deal of money when the City of Glasgow Bank failed in 1878[134] – the word *retribution* comes to mind.

Robert's captaincy of the *Three Bells* on her next trip (to Montreal) had already been advertised but when she arrived in Canada on June 6th 1854, she was commanded by a Mr McCallum. Perhaps Robert was too exhausted to sail again immediately, perhaps he was angry about the money collected in America, possibly both. In a few short weeks he had been within a whisker of both death and wealth, and experienced several other extremes: from the cold of an iron ship in winter to the warmth of Astor House, from shortage of food and water to banqueting on the finest delicacies, from the generosity and gratitude of the Americans to the (apparent) greed of his employers. Perhaps it is not very surprising that he did not command another ship for over a year. During this time his eldest son, also called Robert, was born on May 14th 1854 at Drumtogle, the home of Jane's parents John and Jane Thomson.

When he was ready to return to the sea, Robert commanded the iron sailing ship *Tornado* on three voyages to Australia, carrying emigrants to the goldfields. This was a very lucrative business during the 1850s. In just one month of 1853, 32,000 people braved the long journey in steerage from Liverpool to Australia. The emigrants usually went out on the government-assisted passage scheme and the ships carrying them had to comply with rules introduced from 1840 to reduce the death toll from disease. In theory there had to be a qualified surgeon on board and, from 1852, the food was to be stored cooked rather than raw.

The *Tornado* was the first ship to be chartered by Her Majesty's Commissioners to carry government-assisted emigrants from Glasgow rather than from Liverpool, where well-organised crimps or runners waited to fleece them[135]. A favourite scam was to carry their luggage and not return it until a large payment had been extracted. Directed to the cheapest boarding houses in the city, the emigrants were charged far too much for wretched lodgings and were told they could not board the ship without the 'approved gear'. The runners knew just where to buy this largely unnecessary extra baggage. Naturally, pounds sterling had to be exchanged for Australian dollars – on which a margin of around twenty percent could be made. People were often destitute before they had even left Britain.

To reduce these scams, it was suggested that there should be a depot in Liverpool for those awaiting embarkation but each time the proposal was made, it was defeated. Such a place was set up in Birkenhead in 1852[136] where a concerned wealthy woman (Mrs Chisholm), gave free talks about the best way for the emigrants to equip themselves for their new lives. For example, she suggested that a barrel might be better than a box to contain their belongings because it could be moved easily by rolling and would be more useful on arrival. Cut in half it would provide a washing bowl and a water container, a safe place to confine youngsters out of the rain (!) or a cradle.

The *Tornado* sailed from the Clyde on February 17th 1855 with fifteen cabin passengers and 409 people in steerage, of whom 278 were single women (mostly Irish). She was originally commanded by John Brown Teulon, who had a first class certificate, which required extra knowledge of seamanship, navigation and life-saving in the event of a wreck.

The ship was about ninety miles clear of Inishtrahull Island (off the north Coast of Donegal, Ireland) on March 4th when she encountered a fierce gale. The main trussel-tree (framing that holds the topmast to the mainmast, usually made of oak) gave way and there was other damage[137]. Teulon had no choice but to put back for Greenock, where repairs took about five weeks. This must have been hard for the emigrants in steerage, cooped up so near the homes they had left for ever but no further towards their destination on the far side of the world. It was also a large expense for the owners (all that extra food and pay)

By this date, matters of discipline (including the names of deserters), illness and any births or deaths had to be recorded in crew log books that were handed in to the shipping office of the home port at the end of the voyage. Most of the books from this period were destroyed, but some for the *Tornado* survive. They give an interesting insight into some aspects of life on board from the captain's point of view.

From the log book of the *Tornado*[138]:

1855
March, Greenock (commanded by Captain Teulon)
Having given George Ewing seaman 3 days liberty on the 12th inst, and in not returning up to this date, consider him as a deserter from the ship

March 26th
Having found Mr Mackay, Second Mate and Hugh Quinn, Boatswain in a state of inebriation, unfit for duty, sent them on shore

March 29th
Discharged the Second Mate and Boatswain from the ship

Notice in the Births section of the *Glasgow Herald* for April 2nd:

> *On 30th ult on board the Tornado off Greenock, the wife of Captain John Brown Teulon, a daughter.*

Mr Teulon made no further entries in the log book so perhaps either mother or baby was not fit to continue with the voyage. For whatever reason Robert took over the command. He had recently passed the examination for his Master's Certificate, awarded on February 19th, even though in theory he did not need to do so. The address he gave was 17 Paterson Street, Glasgow, which no longer exists. The *Tornado* set sail with her new master on April 14th.

From the log book:

> *April 19th*
> *William Browen seaman unfit for duty with pains. Gave him a dose of castor oil and clover's powder. (No surgeon on board, apparently)*

> *April 24th*
> *William Browen returned to his duty*

> *14th May*
> *Robert Holden seaman off duty with sore hand. Gave him opening medicine and poultices*

> *May 28th*
> *Robert Holden returned to his duty cured*

> *June 20th*
> *Francis Charles Smith Seaman, coming down from the mizzen top, lost his hold and fell overboard, the ship going at the rate of 11 knots, after an hour under double reef topsail and the night*

very dark. Brought the ship to the wind but could render him
no assistance

The shipboard auction of this man's clothing made £3.17.3d, which would be given to his dependents together with his wages when the ship returned to its home port.

The *Tornado* reached Hobson's Bay, Melbourne on July 14th. A local paper, the *Argus*, reported that 'by courtesy of Captain Crighton of the *Tornado* they had in their possession later English news, being down to 13th April'. The news in question was by then three months old. There are several references to the arrival of the *Tornado* in the *Argus* of July 20, 1855. The first is an advertisement:

Notice – Immigrant ship Tornado
The immigrants of the above ship have been brought into Depot
and will be open for engagement this day at the following hours
The married couples at 10 am
The single women at 11 am
No person will be admitted to the single women's Depot to hire
a servant without an order which can be obtained at this office

It sounds a little like a cattle market but it did bring together those who sought employment and those who needed workers. Near this notice was printed an editorial comment:

We have much pleasure in drawing attention to a letter which
appears in our advertising columns addressed to the captain of
the Tornado, which reflects highly to the credit of all parties
concerned. We understand that the Immigration Board have also
expressed themselves very much gratified with the appearance of
the vessel and the condition of the immigrants.

This is the letter referred to:

To the Commander, officers and Owners of the Clipper ship Tornado of Glasgow:

Gentlemen – We, the undersigned, immigrants aboard the ship Tornado from Glasgow, feel it our duty to express our heartfelt thanks to you for your kindness and gentlemanly behaviour to us whilst on board your ship during her passage from Glasgow to Melbourne; for we believe you have done all in your power to cheer us, and to add to our comforts during the voyage; and we feel we could not have had a pleasanter passage than we have had under your command. And we also thank you on behalf of the owners, for the good and plentiful supply of provisions we have been supplied with; also to her Majesty's Commissioners for chartering such a splendid vessel, but, above all, for the employment of yourself as captain. We have been a long time on board the ship in consequence of the misfortune which compelled us to put back to Greenock. But we believe it was ordained by a wise Providence; and we are glad now we had to return; for, if not, we should not have had the happiness of sailing under your command, for we are satisfied we could not have been better treated than you have done to us. We also thank Mr Davis, the chief mate, and Mr Thomson, second mate, also Mr Burnett the third mate for their kindness and civility to us during our passage; for whether in the rough or fine weather, they were always ready to cheer and enliven us and better officers you could not have had; and we hope that you and they may have a safe and prosperous voyage home, and return to the bosoms of your families in good health, is the fervent wish of Yours respectfully

(The names of one woman and thirty-nine men including Zaccheus F. Fear, Constable!)

Signed on behalf of all the passengers on the Tornado

Conditions in steerage on earlier emigrant ships had been truly appalling: little light or ventilation, a single tap for washing, people having to crawl over each other to get to their bunks, no seating and scarcely-edible food passed around in buckets. Under these conditions many died, frequently of typhus (which is transmitted by lice) and especially children. The *Tornado* clearly provided very much better conditions. Most of those lucky enough to emigrate on her arrived at their destination in a healthy condition and only three died on the voyage. This was less than one percent of the total compared with nearly eighteen percent of those who set off for Canada from the UK in 1848, a much shorter journey.

The log book continued:

July 17th, Hobson's Bay
James Seymour and William Brown deserted from the ship in
a small raft and were picked up by police officers and sentenced
to 12 week's hard labour by the Court

July 18th
John Duncan seaman, off duty, said that he had broken a bone in
his chest. The doctor examined him and said that there was no
bone broken. Duncan said he was not satisfied with his opinion.
The Master told him he could go to any doctor in Melbourne

August 14th
John Duncan went ashore to see the Magistrate and a doctor. He
was ordered on board to his work or else he would be sent to the
hulks, upon which he came on board but would not go to his duty

August 16th
Duncan asked liberty to go ashore to see another doctor but did
not return on board

While at Hobson's Bay eleven more men deserted the ship, four of them in the lighter (a barge). Such desertions were very common because those who could not afford the fare to Australia and were ineligible for a free passage often resorted to this method of getting there. Deserters forfeited their pay and, if apprehended, could be sent to gaol for three months with hard labour. Sometimes desertions reduced the crew so much that manning the ship for the return journey was a problem.

Robert's fame eventually caught up with him. On August 20th, the *Tornado* was cleared outwards for the crossing from Melbourne to Calcutta and there appeared a paragraph in several Australian newspapers pointing out that 'Captain Creighton, at present in command of the *Tornado* is the gentleman who rescued so many people from the *San Francisco*.' Some Americans living in Melbourne held a dinner for him to 'testify their sense of his gallant services to their countrymen'[139].

There were eighteen cabin passengers on the return voyage and 5419 ounces of gold (153.6 kilos, worth roughly £3.8 million in February 2014) in the hold.

The *Tornado* had reached Calcutta by the end of October, where a crewman came to an unfortunate end:

November 1st Calcutta
David Paterson Sailmaker, having been off duty this last two
days with drink, sometime on board and some time on shore. At
9.30 am he was going ashore... and he either fell or jumped off
to the bottom of the dock and must have hurted himself severly.
He was taken to hospital immediately and died on 12th inst.

The log book contains many entries about venereal disease, for which there were then no useful treatments and some harmful ones. Calomel (mercurous chloride) caused the lesions of syphilis to disappear when applied locally, but the disease was not cured and would emerge later in the secondary or tertiary phase. Mercury is highly poisonous[140] and thought to be responsible for many deaths before its medical use disappeared entirely *in the 1960s.*

Robert sent two sailors with 'the venereal disease' to hospital in Calcutta. They returned to work, apparently cured, three weeks later, just before the *Tornado* sailed during the last week in November. Very soon afterwards, crew member James Lockett developed a fever which Robert treated with 'emetic, castor oil and quinine'. Lockett returned to duty very briefly in December but became ill again. On close questioning he admitted having syphilis and said he thought it would go away. Robert then gave him the standard calomel salts, applied a poultice and eventually 'lanced it' (ouch!) Lockett did not return to work until January 23rd. Another sailor, Thomas Linsley, was treated for the same problem with calomel, clover powder salts and lancing.

When Robert handed the completed log book to the port authorities of Liverpool (not Glasgow) on March 27th 1856, he had been away for nearly a year.

The crew agreement and log book for Robert's second voyage with the *Tornado* also survive[141]. The instructions emphasise Robert's responsibility to find and purchase the cargo for the return journey and determine the route home:

Liverpool to Melbourne then (if required) to any ports and places in the Pacific Ocean, Indian or China seas or wherever freight may offer and back to a final port in the United Kingdom for a term not to exceed three years.

'No grog allowed' was added below this. Traditionally grog was made with weak beer and rum, in some ships lime juice was added to guard against scurvy.

Jane (and almost certainly the two children) were with Robert when the *Tornado* set sail from Liverpool on 7th June, 1856. This journey was very different from Jane's previous journey on the *Zarah* because now there were fourteen cabin passengers to be entertained and her own lively children to be kept safe and happy. The cargo weighed over two thousand tons: soap, saddlery, earthenware, butter, ham, pork, bacon, oats, cheese, salt, rice, beer, brandy, candles, spades, forks, nails, axles, a considerable amount of 'soft goods' (fabric and clothes), flagstones and 30,460 slates[142]. Not surprisingly, the ship was very low in the water.

On 30th August there was a potentially very serious situation:

Latitude 42'10' S 10'0' E (mid-Atlantic, south and west of the Cape of Good Hope)

Mr Johnson, Chief Officer, watch on deck. I gave him the order to haul the mainsail up and stow it at 12 hours it then blowing hard. Mr Johnson came aft on the poop and told me the crew refused to stow it. Immediately went forward to the forecastle taking the second officer with me and found John Mathieson belonging to Mr Johnson's watch sitting on a chest at the forecastle doo[r]. Requested him to go out and furl the mainsail when he put his hands across his breast and distinctly told me he would not. I then came aft and called all hands aft and explained the offence they were committing in disobeying a lawful command. I then put the question to John Mathieson (as he had been the first to refuse me) would he go and assist in furling the main sail when he answered he would not. I then gave a general order for all hands to lay aloft and furl the main sail, when they all went. Mathieson saying at the same time that he would go to[o] but I answered him No as it was too late. I then ordered the Chief Officer that Mathieson should do no more work on board the ship Robt Crighton Master

John Mathieson was later sentenced to one month's confinement by the magistrate at Williamstown, Melbourne. Robert's actions seem well-judged and fair.

The elements had not yet finished with them[143]:

The Tornado captained by our old friend Captain Crighton who, it may be remembered, was instrumental in saving a great many lives when in command of the Three Bells, arrived on Wednesday after what might be considered a very fair run, the vessel being very deeply laden, bringing over 2000 tons of cargo. She lost topmast trussel-trees [again!] in 37 South 28 West and was in consequence in want of any sails on the main mast for six days, blowing a string breeze from the NW, but the ship being so deep it was impossible to work on deck: the sea breaking all over it, the men were not able to work

The position is in the Pacific Ocean, to the south-east of South Africa. They arrived at Melbourne on September 11th where the cargo was advertised for sale, including: 'Cheese, Ham and Bacon in splendid condition ex-*Tornado*' and ten cases of 'Superior full shaft saddles with rings, dees and staples complete' and some bridles. There was an auction of seven thousand pounds worth of 'The most Extensive and Important Shipment of soft goods ever offered for sale in this city'. These included: sheeting, shirting, fringed toilet seat covers, baize, cotton socks, haberdashery, silks, ribbons and muslins. Rather strangely, since wool was usually exported from Australia, another auction house disposed of:

4 bales each 100 x 9lb woolpacks ex-Tornado.
More or less damaged by sea water and to be sold without reserve.

Robert reported the fifteen men who deserted the ship in Melbourne to the authorities, including James Mathieson (brother of John?) and the carpenter Alexander Cumming. Of those who stayed, John Martin was sent to hospital with a swollen knee and John Thomson was treated by a doctor on shore for sore eyes. The steward John Gibb was twice found intoxicated and unfit for duty while in port; he was unable to work from 15th – 20th September.

In spite of the very rough weather the cabin passengers were evidently pleased with the way they had been treated[144]:

To Captain Crighton-

Dear Sir
I have been requested by the lady passengers in the saloon of the Tornado including Mrs Rollo and family to present their sincere thanks to you and Mrs Crighton, and to the officers and stewards of the ship, for the kindness they received during the passage of the Tornado from Liverpool to Melbourne. They desire me to assure you that they enjoyed every comfort and attention they could desire and feel grateful for the strict order, propriety and harmony which through your judicious management prevailed among the passengers and officers of the ship during the voyage; and to express their satisfaction as to the quantity and quality of the provisions with which they were supplied.
Wishing you every success in your profession, health and happiness

I remain, dear Sir
Your most obedient servant
J.B.Rollo

Robert was eager to sail for home in October 1856 but could not do so until the first week of November, when he had managed to recruit a sufficient crew. The *Tornado* was carrying mail for her first port of call and ten thousand gold sovereigns[145].

She arrived at Point de Galle in Ceylon on December 20th and sailed for Bombay on Christmas Day. Jane gave birth to her third child, a boy, at sea on January 6th 1857; she must have been in the early stages of pregnancy when they left Liverpool. At Bombay John Gibb was found intoxicated again on January 12th and returned to duty on 13th 'in a muddled state'. The new baby was baptised John Thomson in St. Andrew's Presbyterian Church on February 9th and while in port Robert had treatment for an 'inflammation of the spleen and stomach' which 'did no good at all'[146].

The Anglo-Persian War had begun in the same week that the *Tornado* left Australia for home. Herat, a previously independent city in Afghanistan, was overrun by the Persians and the British authorities regarded this as a threat to British India. When the Persians refused to withdraw, the Governor General of India declared war (November 1st 1856). He was acting on orders from London and this round-about procedure was intended to deflect criticism from the Prime Minister, Lord Palmerston. Memories of the recent, disastrous Crimean War were still fresh. East India Company troops sent from Bombay quickly took the towns of Bulshire, Mohammerah and Ahraz and defeated the Persians at Khoosh-Ab. The Treaty of Paris that ended the war was signed on March 4th 1857[147].

Meanwhile, the Company soldiers and their supplies were needed back in India as soon as possible due to increasing unrest in the army there. The very unhealthy climate in the Gulf was also a cause for concern. Merchant ships in the area were chartered as transports and this was good business for their owners because they were generously compensated. The *Tornado* was not only already on the scene; she had berths for hundreds of soldiers and cabin accommodation for their officers. She and the *Julia* were despatched for Mohammerah in the Persian Gulf on March 11th.

The *Tornado* was back by the end of April. In Bombay Robert wrote that John Gibb was intoxicated on the 25th, 26th and 30th of that month. His patience was exhausted; when Gibb got drunk again on May 1st he was sent ashore to be discharged. The soldiers on board were ordered to Calcutta immediately on landing[148]. There was tension in the air.

Having broken out in Meerut on May 10th, the Indian Mutiny was already under way when Robert sailed for Mohammerah again on May 23rd. He may have felt that it was safer and more comfortable for Jane and the children to stay in Bombay while he was in the Gulf – the Mutiny was still a long way away. During this voyage several of the *Tornado*'s crew suffered from severe fever followed by boils, treated by Robert:

May 26th
Alex Horwood off duty with fever gave him fever mixture then
quinine, Afterwards he came out all in boils from the head to the
foot. I applied poultices keeping his bowels open with medicine
but he got so weak I had to keep his strength up with port wine
which cured him

Those with 'bilious attacks' were medicated somewhat less enjoyably:

June 4th-9th
James McIndoe off duty with severe bilious attack, gave him first
emetick, then Blue pills with salts after these when he recovered

Blue pills were an anti-syphilitic made from corrosive sublimate, a compound of mercury.

The *Tornado* returned to Bombay with soldiers and their equipment on September 27th. There is a poignant reminder in the log book of the dangers faced by sailors:

Bombay October 10th 1857
John Steel AB when out on the maintopsail yard unreving
maintopsail sheet missed his hold and fell upon deck striking the
main yard in his fall. On going to him immediately found life to
be extinct. 2pm took the body on shore where a Coroner's inquest
was held. Verdict accidentally killed by a fall from the maintopsail
yard of the English ship 'Tornado'. Buried him 30th October[149].

John was only twenty-five years old. His clothes, box and Bible were sold for £2.0.0 on the way home. This and his accumulated pay (less what he had been advanced) of £20/17/2d would be kept at the shipping office in the home port, to be claimed by a relative.

The *Tornado* finally left Bombay for the United Kingdom about December 1st, 1857, good news for the owners of the gold sovereigns in her hold (unless they had already been passed on to another ship). Jane was probably very pleased to be on the way home at last. After replenishing supplies at St Helena, the *Tornado* reached Liverpool on April 3rd having been away for twenty-two months, far longer than the usual time for a voyage to Australia.

However, a sailor's life was at sea and on May 20th 1858, Robert began his last command of the *Tornado*. Jane stayed at home, she was pregnant again and the two older children were of school age. The family may have gone to stay with Jane's parents on the farm at Auchterader, where her fourth child was born.

We are fortunate that the outward journey was recorded by Benjamin Gilmore Wilson, one of the cabin passengers[150]. Wilson came from a large Irish farming family and had emigrated to England to escape the 'dark, dark days of our trouble', by which he presumably meant the potato famine. A Baptist Minister who had also studied homeopathic medicine, he volunteered to take charge of the first Baptist Church in Brisbane, Queensland, at one-sixth of his previous salary and boarded the *Tornado* at Liverpool with his wife and two children.

After leaving on May 20th, the tug boats struggled for two days against a strong headwind to clear the *Tornado* out of the River Mersey. Many passengers were seasick and must have wondered how they were going to survive the next few months. One of ship's owners returned to port with the tugs, but not before Mr Wilson had overheard a revealing conversation:

> *[The owner gave] instructions to the purser outside my cabin-door that has made me feel as if every passenger on board was looked upon by him as something out of which he could make as much as possible. 'Be civil and courteous' he said to the purser, 'but keep back all you can'.*

For another two days they sailed 'beautifully' and even saw a porpoise but, on May 25th, scarlatina broke out. Robert related the symptoms suffered by two-year-old John Burns to Mr Wilson, who said he was certain the boy would die – which he did the next morning. The Minister officiated at the funeral service and 'committed his body to the deep'.

Many more passengers became ill (though not all with scarlatina) as did Robert. The doctor, who Mr Wilson described as 'a very feeble old man', was also suffering. The ship's owners had employed him and supplied a chest so 'ill-provided with medicines that if sickness should break out in the vessel he could not meet the wants of the patients'. Dr Charles Phillips was actually seventy-four years old but had put '60' in the age column when he signed the crew agreement in a shaky hand[151]. Clearly, the *Tornado*'s owners were cutting costs wherever they could and had fallen very much in Mr Wilson's estimation since he 'learned this with other not very creditable matters from various sources'. He does seem to have been a bit of a gossip.

Mr Wilson thought it a privilege to be acquainted with Robert, who was 'like a father to us all' and with whom he talked about religious subjects. Taking over from the official doctor, he treated the sick who were all better by May 29th.

A child with whooping cough developed fits and Mr Wilson gave him drops of belladonna (from the plant deadly nightshade, poisonous in larger amounts) and 'a spoonful of water'. Although the boy was apparently better, the old doctor insisted on painting his mouth and throat with croton oil, a long-past-its-use-by date treatment which incensed Mr Wilson. Later the child's father refused to allow Dr Phillips near his son, which is not surprising because the oil is very irritating and painful and causes diarrhoea even in small amounts. Others begged the parson to treat them, which he did, refusing any payment.

By June 3rd, the boy with whooping cough had recovered but the doctor was considerably worse and could hardly walk. Mr Wilson thought him 'the most infirm medical man' he had ever encountered and that it must have been plain to the owners that the doctor they had appointed was entirely unsuitable for his position on the *Tornado*. Two days later the old man was better but had 'got into an awful mess with the passengers, which has greatly grieved the Captain'. The nature of the 'mess' was not explained.

On June 6th Robert showed the cabin passengers where to look for Madeira, a distant speck thirty-five miles from the ship. It was a Sunday, when the decks were cleared for one or more services (called 'rigging church'). All available crew had to attend, washed, shaved and in clean clothes, or be fined. Any clerical gentleman could officiate or the captain might read from the Bible and say some prayers. Not everyone was happy about this; one man, referred to only as Mr B, remarked loudly that he would hang a parson a week and a bishop a month if he could. Just two days later Mrs B somewhat bare-facedly came to see Mr Wilson, saying her husband was very ill and wanted his advice! In true Christian spirit the parson went to see Mr B and prescribed some medicine. He got his reward the next Sunday when the couple attended the service in their best clothes and paid attention to his sermon.

There was a certain amount of horse-play among the younger passengers, who were no doubt bored by this time. An occupant of Cabin Two had his face 'bedaubed' with treacle and was otherwise ill-used, for which he had complained to the captain. This was not a good idea; the next day he found his bed ripped up. Robert could not discover who was responsible and threatened to stop the rations of everyone in the cabin. For some reason (because he was used to dealing with problems alone) he told Mr Wilson of this. The parson offered to speak to the miscreants, which he did with apparently excellent results.

Mr Wilson was clearly a man of ideas and considerable energy. In mid-June he called a meeting of the ministers on board to which Robert was invited. He suggested that the saloon passengers 'should give the sailors a treat by having a tea meeting' followed by a public meeting for the mutual enjoyment and profit of all. This was held to be an excellent idea and planning began, but Robert was indisposed:

June 19ᵗʰ
An interview today with the Captain. I find him ill and suffering from bad treatment of the same illness, inflammation of the spleen and stomach, in India. He places himself entirely under my treatment. Lord direct me how to use the proper remedies.

His prayer was granted and Robert's health improved. Mr Wilson cannot have been universally popular because three of the saloon passengers opposed his tea meeting and proposed a counter one of their own. Robert did not consent to this and the suggestion was quietly buried. Tea, sugar and flour for spice cakes were ordered, together with 'a plum pudding for the sailor's tea'. The crew were invited personally by the ministers. Mr Wilson did not record their reactions but, even if the sailors would have preferred a less formal occasion with alcohol rather than tea, the meeting promised a welcome break from routine and cakes were a rare treat.

Mr B was still in trouble. He fell onto a cannon and hurt himself so badly that 'he was carried in in a fainting state. His wife who had so far given us such wicked annoyance came running to me crying and beseeching me aid on behalf of her husband'. The good parson applied arnica (still used for bruising) and the patient recovered sufficiently to attend the tea meeting a few days later. This was a resounding success. Robert took the chair; there was music (the saloon had a piano) and singing between the speeches, which included a vote of thanks to the captain, heartily endorsed by loud cheering. Thanking Mr Wilson, Robert said he was so delighted with the entertainment that he would try to have something similar organised on future voyages. The tea meeting may be the first recorded instance of an on-board entertainment given by the passengers for the sailors.

By now, the *Tornado* was about half way to her destination and time began to hang heavily. Robert taught the parson how to use the quadrant and pointed out a whale blowing in the distance, 'what an enormous beast he seems in the water'. Sadly, one of the younger sailors died of scarlet fever on July 8th.

One week later a tremendous storm hit the ship. The gale sent one of the booms (a sail-carrying spar) crashing down onto the deck, breaking Joseph Witty's arm and injuring his face. The doctor set his arm and dressed the wounds but Joseph was not fit to return to duty for three months. Rather more cheerful news was that on July 25th, 'Mrs C.P. Hansen was delivered of a son'[152].

The *Tornado* berthed at Melbourne on August 20th where twenty-one of the crew deserted. Two were discharged and so would receive their pay. The next day, Mr Wilson's family left the ship to begin their new lives. He found the local Baptist Church and climbed over the rails because the gate was locked. Perhaps there were a lot of criminals about[153].

The diary gives a fascinating glimpse into Robert's life. He dealt firmly with troublemakers, had a long-standing stomach complaint and took time to talk to the passengers, even teaching Mr Wilson how to use a quadrant.

Several advertisements for cargo and passengers for the return journey, with a departure date in November, appeared in the local newspapers but the *Tornado* did not sail until late December for lack of these and sufficient crew. Twenty men were signed on in Melbourne on December 13th.

Eagle Line of Packets[154]
Ship Tornado Captain Crighton for Liverpool. All accounts against this vessel must be sent to the office of the undersigned before 12 o'clock THIS DAY or they will not be recognised.
The clipper ship Tornado has room for a limited quantity of WOOL, which will be taken at the lowest current rate for freight.
The clipper ship Tornado still has some first-rate BERTHS for which immediate application is necessary as the ship will sail on Saturday December 11[th.]
GOLD will be weighed up to Friday December 10[th.]
Notice to Passengers. All BALANCES to be PAID UP by Friday morning December 10th.

Eventually Robert (or the agents) collected ten cabin-class passengers and thirty in the second and intermediate classes together with plenty of cargo[155]:

Exports, Tornado Creighton for Liverpool.
1291 bales of wool 120 tons bark 1 chronometer
37 bales of sheep skins 5380 bags copper ore 8 boxes private effects
11 bales of leather 147 bags scrap iron 2969 railway sleepers
14 casks of tallow 3 boxes apparel 1 case ploughs
24 packages of gold belonging to six banks.

To carry such a valuable cargo was risky. In October 1848, three sailors on the *Amelia* (not the same one Robert once commanded) murdered their captain, both mates and a passenger in order to steal the £300,000 in gold and silver in her hold. (Although they did not escape with it. Some plucky junior crew members waited until the mutineers drank themselves insensible, killed them and managed to reach safety – in spite of their lack of navigation skills.)[156]

The *Tornado* sailed on December 23rd in company with the *Saldanha* and the *Morning Light*, all bound for Liverpool, although Hobson's Bay had been hit by a gale that 'did great damage to shipping' a few days previously.

Having such valuable cargo certainly created extra interest in a ship's progress. The *Morning Light* arrived in Liverpool on March 19th but Robert's ship was somewhat overdue:

The arrival of the Tornado from Melbourne with 116,600l[157] in gold is now daily looked for this vessel having been at sea 100 days.

She was off Holyhead on the 25th March 1859 and reached Liverpool the next day. 'The gold brought by the *Tornado* was taken for the Continent' [158] is the only further reference to the cargo. It was probably only then that Robert learned he had a third son, Charles Edward Crighton, born at his grandparent's farm the previous December.

Joseph Witty, of the broken arm, was one of the very few ordinary seamen who stayed with the *Tornado* for her whole round trip. His pay for the ten months would have been either £15 or £30 (depending on age), in contrast to the value of the gold that he had helped to transport. A letter from Robert was tucked into the crew agreements shows that an apprentice would have received only ten shillings for the whole journey:

Liverpool 19th April /59
Captain Quinby (?) Shipping Master

Sir
In reply to your enquiry why the desertions of William Henry
Caton & Samuel Thrower [apprentices] at Melbourne are not
(endorsed ?) – I beg to stat[e] that they left the vessel just as I
was sailing. Consequently I had not an opportunity of reporting
them. With regard to the other three they shipped at a normal
wage of 1/ – per month they left the ship upon arrival and did
not appear to be discharged.
I am Sir Your Obedient servant
Robt Crighton Comder Ship Tornado.

The *Tornado* was next advertised as sailing to New Zealand[159]:

White Star Line
The magnificent clipper Tornado Captain Crighton will be
despatched for Auckland and Wellington on 10th June. She is
one of the finest and fastest clippers afloat and has splendid
accommodation in the poop for a large number of saloon
passengers for whose accommodation is provided a piano, library,
bedding linen and all necessities.
The arrangements for 2nd cabin, intermediate and steerage passengers
are equal to those of any ship afloat, the between decks are nearly
nine feet high, beautifully lighted and thoroughly ventilated.

However, when the *Tornado* sailed on the advertised day, her commander was not Robert but a James Aitken. As well as 280 passengers, she carried forty thousand 'Best Blue Bangor Countess Slates', a hundred and eighty tons of Welsh steam-coal and a 'Pure Bred Short Horned Cow, Lucy'.

The White Star Line owners might have done better to retain Robert as captain, if he could have been persuaded to stay. On arrival at New Zealand some of the *Tornado*'s passengers were not at all happy and, on October 7th, Captain Aitken appeared before a judge in Auckland for breach of contract[160]. A saloon passenger, backed up by a colleague, alleged that the passengers had not been provided with adequate provisions while in port. There was also considerable argument about whether their tickets onward to Wellington were valid or not. They had originally been made out for Auckland and the word 'Wellington' had been inserted after the contract had been signed. The purser of the *Tornado* would not 'swear that I did not use the word forgery'. Both sides gave their version of what food had been served, the passengers claiming that raw pork had been served on two days and nothing on another. It was agreed the cook had been drunk. The Judge found the evidence contradictory and dismissed the claim, saying that, while the tickets were not lawful, it 'was not the Captain's fault'.

Although Wellington had been advertised as a destination, the *Tornado* did not sail there but left Auckland for Callao (Peru) and Lima on November 2nd 1859 in ballast with just three passengers. After discharging the passengers she was loaded with guano and sailed for the United Kingdom, but was wrecked in the notoriously dangerous Strait of Magellan. Luckily, the crew were rescued[161]:

Her Majesty's ship Mutine arrived at Valparaiso on June 25th from Rio de Janeiro bringing with her the crew of the ship Tornado of Glasgow, Captain Aitken which sailed with guano from Callao for Queenstown on April 1st last. She was an iron vessel of 1229 tons register built... in 1853.

Robert had relinquished his command in time, though he probably would have chosen a different route home. This last voyage of the

Tornado had been advertised with him in command and, from how he signed his letter (about the apprentices) to the Liverpool Shipping Office, he clearly regarded himself as her captain until at least April 19th. Yet on May 17th he applied for a replacement Master's Certificate from a Glasgow address and four days later set sail on a ship of a different line. His plans may have changed when he discovered that the *Tornado*'s new destination was New Zealand, which would mean a very long separation from his family. He might also have been concerned about the increasing parsimony of the ship's owners. Ships with steam engines and sails were gradually taking over from those relying on wind power alone and it was becoming increasingly difficult to make a profit from a sailing ship. Their crews were being reduced alongside other cost-cutting measures. As we have seen, on her previous voyage the *Tornado*'s owners had ordered the purser to 'keep back as much as possible' and had employed a very old (cheap) doctor. Perhaps they were demanding further, unpalatable, economies.

Robert's timing was good. The magnificent *John Bell* of the Anchor Line was about to ply the Atlantic from Glasgow. Who better to command her than a man well-known and admired in America, especially by those who selected the ships to carry their merchandise?

Chapter Eight
The *John Bell*

The *John Bell* started life in May 1854 as a full-rigged clipper[162]. Built at Govan, she was named for the man who owned half the shares in her (ships were commonly owned by consortia, to spread the risk). John Bell was one of the three men who owned the *Three Bells,* who may have misappropriated the money collected for Robert in America. If they did so, he must have either forgiven them or decided that the past was the past.

After two round trips to Australia during the time Robert was commanding the *Tornado*, the *John Bell* returned to Glasgow in late 1856. She was fitted with a screw propeller and auxiliary engines[163], enabling a speed of nine knots without sails and leased to Messrs Handyside and Henderson of the Anchor Line. Destined for the transatlantic trade, she was instead chartered by the East India Company as a troop carrier when the Indian Mutiny broke out in 1857[164]. After the Rebellion ended in 1858 (taking both the Company and the Mughal Empire with it), the *John Bell* began plying the Atlantic with the Anchor Line. She was refitted to carry passengers and cargo to Québec and Montreal in the summer (when the St. Lawrence River was ice-free) and to New York in winter. The round trips took less than two months, which would allow Robert to see more of his family.

The change of employer was not without a final glitch; Robert could not produce his Master's Certificate. On 17th May 1859 he wrote to the port authorities of Glasgow requesting a replacement, quoting his address as Paisley Road, Glasgow[165]:

I hereby sincerely and solemnly declare that the circumstances under which I lost my certificate of Competency as set forth on your (?Books) are strictly true (signed)

The new paperwork was issued on 19th May and, two days later the *John Bell* left the Clyde for Canada with passengers and a cargo of manufactured goods. Readers of the *Glasgow Herald* were reminded that her commander was the same man who had rescued 'the passengers... of the American ill-fated steamer *San Francisco*'. The forty members of the *John Bell*'s crew included a surgeon, eight stewards, two cooks, a baker and six firemen (stokers). Seamen and firemen had to agree to 'trim coal' (stow it evenly throughout the ship) as required and everyone had to report sober at the time stated or the master 'may ship others in their place.' The pay list survives, in Robert's handwriting; unfortunately it does not include his salary[166]. There is also a list of fines for specific offences including one day's pay for 'smoking below', insolence or swearing, not attending Divine Service (unless ill or on duty) or 'not being clean, shaved and washed on Sunday'. 'Secreting contraband with intent to smuggle' incurred a fine of a month's pay and a cook who did not have meals ready for the crew at the appointed time lost a day's money. The fines were doubled for officers.

The *John Bell* reached Québec after nineteen days at sea and continued to Montreal where there was a little trouble with the chief steward-

From the log book:

11th June 1859 Montreal
Gave orders to James Fleming, Chief Steward, to get his cabins in order for the inspection of passengers. Instead of doing which he went on shore about 11 am and did not return until 4 pm when he came on board intoxicated and gave insolence. For which I put him off duty.

Signed by Robert Crighton (master), John Kincaid Lennox (surgeon) and John H. Caverley (purser).

Fleming was given two day's leave to look for another situation, but had to return to the ship when he could not find one. Robert reduced him to steward of the fore cabin and ordered him back to work.

The *John Bell* was back in the Clyde on 6th July, having taken only fourteen days and sixteen and a half hours on the return journey. This was despite a delay of eighteen hours off the coast of Newfoundland due to 'a large field of ice' and strong easterlies during the last part of the voyage. Before going ashore, each man signed off (literally, making a mark if he could not write) while Robert remained on board to do the paperwork, which included grading the crew's skill and conduct. Almost everyone got 'VG' (very good) for seamanship and behaviour, except James Fleming and one other man who were given 'I' (indifferent) for sobriety, the lowest grade. The twenty cabin passengers had enjoyed their experience:[167]

We, the undersigned passengers by the steamship John Bell, under your command, have great pleasure in expressing to you our admiration of your conduct in caring for our safety and comfort during the voyage which has now terminated. We feel it would be presumptuous in us to hazard an opinion regarding the management of the ship. Nevertheless we are satisfied from the way in which the orders were given and obeyed that our safety under the blessing of God was in the hands of a most experienced and skilful commander. Your gentlemanly bearing and considerate kindness to all, and especially to those suffering from sickness we shall ever remember with gratitude and respect. We are happy to say that throughout the voyage we have heard no improper language by either officers or crew – for our entire freedom from this too-frequent annoyance to travellers, we are

*persuaded we owe much to your influence and example. We desire
to express through you our obligations to the Surgeon, Purser and
Officers for their urbanity and attention to us on all occasions.
Some of us may mention, started earlier on this voyage than we
had intended for the sake of directly reaching the port to which
you were to sail, but now we beg unfeignedly to assure you that,
were it to begin again, we would hasten or postpone it in order
that we might enjoy the pleasure of your society, and the feeling
of security which your command has imparted.*

*Wishing you every happiness in your family, great success in your
profession and, when the voyage of life is ended, a safe entrance
into the haven of rest*

We remain Yours Very Respectfully

(all the cabin passengers.)

A happy ship is a well-disciplined ship. It is clear that Robert
expected very high standards of those who worked for him and did
not tolerate drunkenness, bad language or insolence. This address
from satisfied passengers would also 'doubtless remind many of our
readers of the high character and abilities of the man, as exemplified
on a more trying occasion'. Robert's heroism had not yet been entirely
forgotten.

The ship left Glasgow again for Canada on 15ᵗʰ July with James
Fleming, somewhat surprisingly, employed as first steward. Two of
the crew deserted at Montreal, taking all their belongings with them
and Charles Webb was fined for refusing to 'holleystone' the deck
in pouring rain. On hearing this, he originally refused to work at
all, but reconsidered his position and had 'returned to duty' by the
end of the day.

Not all of a captain's duties were to do with discipline, Robert
had a much happier one to perform:

Marriages[168]

At Montreal, on board the steamer John Bell, on the 3ʳᵈ instant, by the Rev Professor Young, of Knox College, Toronto, the Rev. D.E.Montgomery M.A. of the Free Church, South Gower, to Jane, eldest daughter of Captain Richard Rennie, Fifeshire Royal Artillery, Glasgow, Scotland.

At Montreal, on board the steamer John Bell on the 3ʳᵈ instant, by the Rev D.E.Montgomery, of the Free Church, South Gower, J.K.Edwards, M.A., editor of the Montreal Transcript, to Jane Somers, eldest daughter of the late Colin Galbraith, writer, Edinburgh, Scotland . The two brides were given away by Captain Crighton, commander of the John Bell.

The day before these marriages took place, seaman William Beck was taken to hospital with smallpox. This must have been extremely worrying. Smallpox is highly contagious, with an incubation period of about twelve to fourteen days and a mortality rate of about thirty per cent. Beck's clothes should have been burned because the virus can live for up to a week outside the body. It is greatly to the surgeon's credit that no further instances occurred; he probably isolated Beck and all his belongings as soon as the characteristic symptoms of the disease developed. A note of actions taken, written on Anchor Line notepaper and signed by the surgeon, was kept with the crew agreement in case William Beck's family later enquired about him. Fortunately, his death was not recorded in 1859 in Montreal so he survived the ordeal. There were several hospitals in Canada at that time for the poor: sailors, soldiers, recent immigrants and others without a family home. The patients, mostly suffering from infectious diseases and malnutrition, paid little or nothing for their treatment because the hospitals were charitably funded with some intermittent government aid. They were better than the streets but the dirt and overcrowding made them perfect places for infections to flourish.

When the *John Bell* sailed again from Clydeside on 10th September, for the first time the crew agreement included having to wear the company's uniform 'as required'. On arrival at Montreal one sailor was reported for deserting the ship. In addition:

10th October The effects of Andrew Lyle, seaman are here entered having been put on board by him at Glasgow but failed to sail with the vessel. It is thought he entered her Majesty's Navy on or about 10th September. His effects delivered to the shipping Master at Glasgow.

1 check shirt 1 vest and blanket 1 jumper 2 singlets 9 pairs drawers 1 trousers 1 braces 1 stockings 1 jacket 2 kerchiefs 1 book

With the exception of the underwear (and how did Lyle manage without it?), that hardly seems an adequate wardrobe for weeks at sea.

The ship was overdue by several days on the return journey because they experienced severe weather and violent easterly gales the whole way. The *John Bell* 'behaved admirably throughout', even through the thirty-six hours of a 'hurricane or cyclone [of] unremitting fury'[169]. They reached Liverpool on November 3rd and Robert stayed on board for two days dealing with the paperwork. He added a note to the crew log book that Donald McKay was not competent for the duty of able seaman, as he had claimed, and reduced his pay from £3/15/0 a month to £3/0/0.

That was the last trip of the year to Canada. The *John Bell* sailed for New York on November 11th with a cargo of manufactured goods and 'a fair complement of passengers for the season of the year'. They encountered a strong headwind the whole way and did not arrive until Sunday, December 4th. An American reporter sent to meet Robert aboard his ship found that he had 'fleshed up much since his visit six years since, having become quite portly in appearance. He has still all the cordiality of a bluff, generous sailor[170]'.

Ashore Robert was warmly welcomed by the merchants of the

Corn Exchange and secured almost all the freight for his return journey in a single day. The *John Bell* returned to Glasgow on December 27th with passengers and a large cargo of American produce.

Charles Darwin's newly published book *On the Origin of Species* would have made a fine present for Robert that year if Christmas had been celebrated in Scotland at the time, but the holiday and 'all observation thereof' was still forbidden by an Act of the Scottish Parliament of 1640. The traditional festivities gradually crept back but Christmas Day was not made a public holiday in Scotland until 1958, followed by Boxing Day in 1974. However, Robert was home in time for the traditional Hogmanay celebrations, bringing in the New Year of 1860. Because he was tall and dark he would have been an ideal 'first-footer', carrying health and prosperity across his own and neighbouring thresholds in the form of coal, whisky and black bun.

He had a month at home to see the children before the *John Bell* left the Clyde again for New York on February 1st 1860 with twelve passengers. She had to put back to Queenstown (Ireland) because her shaft and propeller had been lost[171], which was not uncommon in the early days of screw propulsion. Ships of the Twin Screw Line were fitted with two shafts and propellers in order to attract customers who did not want to suffer these delays. Breakdown was usually caused by mechanical failure, brought about by bad weather. When a ship pitched in heavy seas the propeller was sometimes lifted out of the water. This caused it to race, putting a considerable strain on the shaft and couplings. The repairs took several weeks and the *John Bell* did not reach New York until March 29th. The *Washington Evening Star* of April 2nd mentions that 'Capt. Robt. Creighton' was at Willards, which was (and is) a prestigious hotel in the city. He was back on Clydeside by April 27th 1860.

The *John Bell* continued to cross and recross the Atlantic and Robert was advertised as her captain for a few more weeks, but he had started a new career and for the next seven years was a land-based ship's agent, living with his family.

Chapter Nine
Govan, Liverpool and the Last Commands

Govan, home to Rangers Football Club and the (fictional) hard-drinking, unemployed-and-proud-of-it Rab C. Nesbitt, is a district of Glasgow across the Clyde from the city. The first Govan shipyard was established by Napier in 1841 and soon there was a large and growing shipbuilding industry providing plenty of employment, though at a price. Six days a week the noise in the yards was literally deafening. The workers used sign language and learned to lip read as they gradually lost their hearing. The roaring fires of the riveters and 'caulkers and burners' (welders) lit the dullest winter days and baked them in summer, while the crash of hammers on white-hot rivets and of chisel on iron created a wall of sound that knocked a stranger backwards. Respiratory disease was rife and killed many, but it was work and it paid the bills.

Robert moved his family close to this vision of hell in 1860[172] and started his new career as a ship broker, mediating between the builders and buyers of ships, chartering vessels and arranging the buying and selling of cargoes. This was just in time to see the launch of the *Black Prince*, the largest ship then built on Clydeside. The Crightons lived in Lendal Place, a street of traditional three or four storey tenements built of red sandstone. Their house (number 4) still exists today, though the area is very run-down. Jane's mother was staying with them early in 1861[173], presumably to help with the new baby (Alexander) and the family had a general servant.

There was a great slump in the transatlantic trade after the American Civil War broke out in that year, which may have been one of the reasons Robert gave up sea-going. It might have also have been responsible for his move to Liverpool, where he was well-known and had many contacts from his time on the *Tornado* and earlier ships. However, this city's trade was badly hit by the war[174] and the establishment of a new business must have been difficult.

Liverpool had long been a great port, built on cotton and (earlier) on the slave trade. It was here the original 'strike' over wages took place in 1775, when sailors of the slave ship *Derby* found they were to be paid £1 a month rather than the agreed £1/10/0 (£1.50). They tore down the *Derby's* rigging ('striking' it), were imprisoned and then rescued by men from other ships. Together the mob attacked the houses of the hated slave merchants and ship's captains until the Dragoons eventually restored order[175].

The family lived across the Mersey from Liverpool in fashionable Rock Ferry, where another boy, William, was born in January 1863[176]. Always known as William Bell Crighton, he was only registered with the first name. During this year Robert finally gave up all claim on the family home in Port Glasgow[177].

Early in 1864, Robert replied to a letter from Stephen C Massett, actor, song-writer and traveller, who was staying in London[178]:

Robt Crighton   *11, Rumford Place*
Ship and Insurance broker   *Liverpool 25ᵗʰ Jany 1864*
Commission Merchant and
Forwarding Agent

My dear Massett
Your welcome note of January 21ˢᵗ only came to hand this morning. I remember you well and will be happy indeed if you will spend an evening or two with us. Only let me know two days before you come as I may be away from home and I should be sorry not to see you. When did you come to this country and if by way of Liverpool why did you not find time to call upon me.

What are you doing in London and if I can be of any service to
you here, please let me know
Trusting you are enjoying good health
I am
Yours most respectfully
Robt Crighton

Massett was born in England but moved to the United States aged seventeen, eventually setting in New York. In his autobiography (published 1863), he describes a day wandering around Liverpool when between ships[179]. He did not like the city at all and presumably wrote to Robert from London in order not to have to repeat the experience! The two may have met on one of Massett's voyages – he wrote a song called *Our Good Ship Sails Tonight* in 1861, but the vessel is not identified.

Robert was, originally at least, prospering in his new career although his original Liverpool partnership with a Mr Roxburg was dissolved in January 1864. The notepaper he used to write to Stephen Massett is expensively embossed and the family were living at 11 George's View, Rock Ferry, a desirable address at the time.

Birkenhead was not always the depressed place that it is today. Once a fishing village, development began in 1824 when fellow Scot John Laird noticed that the water was deeper there than on the Liverpool side of the Mersey. He started a shipyard and built *The Wye*, a pre-fabricated iron lighter (barge) in 1829 and a paddle steamer in 1833. With a full order book and an increasing workforce, John Laird set out to build a town. He and Francis Richard Price (Lord of the Manor of Birkenhead) employed the architect John Gillespie Graham of Edinburgh to draw up the plans. The streets were to be arranged in a grid pattern (as previously designed by Graham for part of Edinburgh's New Town), there would be a large park and a university to rival those of Oxford and Cambridge. Money poured in but the boom was short-lived. This is reflected in the splendid Hamilton Square, which has the highest percentage of Grade 1 listed buildings anywhere in England, where each of the first three sides was less grand in design and cheaper in construction than the previous one. It was not until 1887 that the Square was completed by the Town Hall, a magnificent building of Scottish granite and sandstone[180].

The Crighton family was still growing, in 1864 young Jane finally got a sister called Mary Catharine. There was plenty for the children to explore: the innovative Pleasure Park with its large lakes, trees and lodges, the river's endless procession of ships, tugs and ferries and the first horse-drawn street tramway in Europe, opened in August 1860. Robert was no longer entirely dependent on ships and shipping for his livelihood. There was a notice in the paper about the Scottish Union Fire and Life Insurance Company's quinquennial bonus to be paid in August to all who had life policies and he is listed as an agent[181]. By then the family's address was Hawthorn Villas, Rock Ferry.

Although the American Civil War affected trade in Liverpool, it was not a total disaster for the area. Many famous ships were launched from Lairds, including two for the Confederacy – the United States was eventually awarded three million pounds for the damage inflicted on the Union by these ships because Britain had officially been neutral. And, despite the conflict, there was continued emigration to the United States. Britain still received more than 40% of her grain from the Union due to poor harvests at home, and supplied munitions to both sides – though much more to the North. However, the cotton trade was very badly hit, since little of the raw material could leave the blockaded Southern US ports and the slump in textile manufacture caused great hardship[182].

Sadly Robert and Jane's third son, eight-year-old Charles Edward, died in February 1867 from 'scarletina maligna', a severe and usually fatal form of scarlet fever. It must have been a time of great worry as well as grief, because the disease is infectious. He was buried in

12. Portrait of Robert. Oil; date and artist unknown

Flaybrick Memorial Garden in Birkenhead but there is no extant headstone. By then the family had moved from Hawthorn Villas to a house on the New Chester Road, Tranmere.

In 1868 Robert returned to the sea, this time for the West Indies and Pacific Steamship Company. Formed in Liverpool in 1863, the company had been awarded the Royal Mail contract for Honduras and Mexico. Robert commanded their steamship *Crusader* on a single voyage to the West Indies and New Orleans, returning to Liverpool at the end of March. Cargoes taken to Jamaica at the time on the Company's ships[183] included fabrics and ready-made clothes, patent medicines, perfumes and even wedding-cake ornaments 'which for elegance cannot be excelled'.

Robert's last command was of the Company's steamship *Venezuelan*. They were at Colon (Panama) in May 1868 and returned to Liverpool by early July with hundreds of bags and some barrels of mother-of-pearl and *Murex* (sea snail) shells among the cargo[184]. Collecting all kinds of exotic shells was a favourite pastime of Victorian ladies and reputedly also of sea captains, who certainly had plenty of opportunities to find or buy them.

The ship sailed again on 16th July, bound for Barbados, Venezuela, Colon and Jamaica, which she reached on September 2nd. Robert carried 'full files' of American newspapers (with reports of the terrible earthquakes in Peru, causing 'severe loss of life'[185]) to the Jamaican News Room and the Merchant's Exchange. He was only at Kingston for a single day before leaving for Haiti. He did not stay there long, either, because the capital Port-au-Prince was besieged by rebel forces and there was 'no produce to be had'[186]. Much worse, foreigners were being persecuted, so he left immediately. The *Venezuelan* arrived back in the Mersey on 30th September. There had been little opportunity for buying and loading cargo and a ship in ballast is an unprofitable ship.

Robert set sail again on the *Venezuelan* in October 1868, with the destinations of Haiti, Jamaica, Mexico and Mobile (Alabama). The cargo unloaded at Kingston included cheese, butter, champagne, canned lobster and other luxury items. There was French pomade for gentlemen's hair styling and cosmetics for the ladies. They could dose themselves with European medicines and then eat jams, jellies or biscuits to take away the taste. There were trusses for hernias, gutta-percha for holes in teeth and bunion plasters, also 'a few bells, suitable for chapels or schools'.

The *Venezuelan* left Jamaica on November 10th for Mexico and Mobile and on the way home called at Norfolk, Virginia on January 13th for supplies, particularly of coal[187]. Robert must have received notification that his Congressional Medal had finally been struck because he telegraphed Washington from Norfolk that this would be the best opportunity for a long time for its presentation. The Americans wasted no time and very soon the ship *Mystic* arrived at Norfolk carrying Major-General W.F. Barry (who commanded nearby Fortress Monroe) and two survivors of the *San Francisco* disaster, Sergeant McNamara and Corporal Miller. Asking these two non-commissioned officers to present Robert with his medal was a masterstroke; nothing could have pleased him more[188].

With the band playing and resplendent in their uniforms, the soldiers boarded the *Venezuelan* and were conducted to the captain's splendid cabin. After some preamble, the General got to the heart of his speech:

> *... Such actions, sir, are characteristic of a true man, as well as of a noble-hearted sailor. The fine ship which you now command plainly attests the way in which your worth is recognised at home. Let this medal remind you, sir, that your merit is also appreciated by those who are not your countrymen. I now deliver the medal to you, sir, in the name of the Congress of the United States with my personal wishes that you may live many years to wear the medal and enjoy the recollection of the good deed it commemorates.*

The beautiful box (walnut lined with blue velvet) containing the medal was then passed to the two soldiers, who in turn handed it to Robert. 'Much affected', he spoke briefly:

> *General Barry. I cannot express to you my feelings on this occasion. I have received so many tokens of respect from the Government of the United States for an act which I believe every British seaman would have performed, that on this occasion I am utterly unable in words to express how deep is my gratitude. All I can say now is, that I am obliged to your Government for this kind gift, which I shall ever appreciate; and to you as its representative on this occasion I return my sincere thanks, and let me say, sir, that nothing is so pleasing to me as to see present on this occasion two survivors of the wreck. Again I thank you, sir.*

After thc ceremony canons were fired, the band played *God Save the Queen* and to the sound of loud and lengthy cheering the *Venezuelan* weighed anchor for Liverpool, arriving on February 1ˢᵗ.

Robert commanded the *Venezuelan* twice more, each time to the Virgin Islands, Venezuela, Columbia and Panama. On March 8ᵗʰ 1869, his Congressional Medal was exhibited at the Underwriter's Rooms in Liverpool[189]. The telegram he had sent regarding its presentation suggests he was already thinking of retiring from the sea by January, which he did when the *Venezuelan* reached Liverpool at the end of July.

On August 9ᵗʰ there was a meeting of her owners, the West Indies and Pacific Steamship Company[190]. Profits had fallen considerably due to political difficulties in some countries (such as Robert had found in Haiti) and the increased competition from subsidised British Mail Companies. It was decided that some of the Company's ships had to be sold and as a result they needed fewer captains. Robert did not re-establish himself as a ship's agent, because in the 1871 census he described his occupation as master mariner. The money he had been awarded by the United States Congress would have supported the family for years.

The Crightons moved again, this time to a small terrace house at 21, Victoria Road, Bebington. Jane and Robert's last child Norman Septimus was born on March 14ᵗʰ, 1871 but died aged six months from whooping cough. He had been ill for fourteen days which must have been a terrible time for the family. Whooping cough is a hazard of having older siblings, who usually survive the disease. But a young baby cannot learn to whoop, which is the sound of the sharply indrawn breath after a coughing bout. The birth and death of Norman and the census are (so far) the only printed references to Robert for the years 1870-1873. He had retired from commanding ocean-going ships, but a related and exciting opportunity was about to be offered to him.

Chapter Ten

Antwerp

In March 1841, when Robert was already first mate of the *Helen Hamilton*, a boy was born into a very old Quaker family in Philadelphia. Named Clement Acton Griscom, he was to rise from the lowly position of clerk in the shipping house of Peter Wright & Co to become the first President of the International Mercantile Marine Company, whose creation was described as 'one of the boldest acts of enterprise in American business history.' Although this seems a long way from Birkenhead and the Crighton family's world, Clement Griscom shaped the last few years of Robert's life and influenced the lives of several of his descendants.

A newspaper announced the formation of a new company in April 1872[191]:

> *The International Navigation Company has joined with the Philadelphia Railroad Company to run a first class line of steamships between Philadelphia and a port on the continent of Europe (most probably Antwerp). The steamers will be known as the Red Star Line and will carry 2,500 tons of cargo, between 800-1000 emigrants and 20 cabin passengers. They start in the summer.*
> *Signed, James A. Wright, President, and Clement A. Griscom, Vice President.*

Nine months later there was a further bulletin, referring to the transatlantic trade-

The Liverpool connection, already established and soon to be greatly extended would not, by itself, suffice to enable our foreign commerce to recuperate.

The recuperation was from the effects of the American Civil War and 'our foreign commerce' was the export of wheat, cotton and tobacco and the transportation of increasing numbers of immigrants from all over Europe. The International Navigation Company of Philadelphia collaborated with the Société Anonyme de Navigation Belge Américaine in the formation of the Red Star Line. Antwerp was chosen because of its central position and because the Belgian Government offered the company an exclusive contract to carry mail[192]. The authorities in Antwerp wanted to arrest the port's long, slow decline and exempted the Red Star Line from wharf and other dues. In 1873, they further voted to expand and modernise facilities for the new, prestigious and faster steamers, their motives contrasting with those of a former developer of the port, Napoleon, who saw Antwerp as 'a pistol pointed at the heart of England' and ordered the building of new shipyards and docks earlier in the century. The ships of the Red Star Line would be built in England – at a much lower cost than in America – but be registered in Antwerp and fly the Belgian flag (with the exception of the *Three Bells* after the *San Francisco* rescue[193], only ships built in America could fly the Stars and Stripes).

The company's original plan was to carry emigrants from Europe and return with some passengers and oil in bulk – rather than in barrels as had previously been the practice. The world's very first oil tanker was the SS *Vaderland*, built for the Red Star Line by Palmers of Jarrow on Tyneside and launched in August 1872. The cargo was problematic, however. The Belgians forbade the building of the necessary storage tanks on the quayside at Antwerp and the Americans would not allow passengers to be carried on the same

13. Photograph of Robert as an old man

ships as oil in tanks. The *Vaderland* was therefore modified to take general cargo and considerably more people – about eight hundred emigrants in third class and seventy people in first and second class. She sailed on her maiden voyage on January 20th 1873 from Antwerp via Falmouth and Halifax to Philadelphia with between ninety and one hundred emigrants (fare, thirty dollars), several second and a few first class passengers (fare, one hundred dollars in gold), together with a cargo of chemicals, pig-lead, glass, firearms, paper, dry goods, hemp, skins and pictures.

The Red Star Line added to their fleet. In 1873, the *Abbotsford* and the *Kenilworth* were chartered for the Liverpool service and, on August 2nd the *Kenilworth* left Philadelphia for Liverpool carrying Clement Griscom with his wife, child and a maid[194]: 'he designs spending some time on the Continent' and 'goes out in the general interest of the Company.' Among other business, Griscom was looking for a man he could trust to be Marine Superintendent of the Red Star Line in Antwerp.

The Crighton family were still living in Birkenhead, just across the river from Liverpool where Robert was 'held in the highest respect'[195]. His Congressional Gold Medal had been displayed in the Exchange not many years before and he had worked there as a shipping and insurance agent as well as having previously commanded ships sailing to and from the great port. He had, of course, also rescued the lives of a great many American citizens and had received a tremendous reception in Philadelphia, where the Griscom family lived. Robert fitted the job description perfectly[196]:

A senior master who had retired from the sea, a marine superintendent acted as a kind of 'super-captain' and technical advisor to the owners. Most owners would not be sailors or have any technical knowledge about ships; a superintendent would look after their interests. He would check the ships when they returned to see they were being maintained well and that stores and equipment were being properly accounted for. Sometimes he appointed the masters.

The Crightons arrived in Antwerp in January, 1874[197]. They had moved house many times before but this must have been still more of an upheaval. Their new home was on the Jordaenskaai, part of the quayside road along the River Scheldt. No contemporary buildings have survived in the street but a postcard of 1910 shows terraced houses three or four stories high, their front doors opening directly onto the pavement. There was, and still is, a mile-long, wrought iron covered market along the quayside into which cargoes were unloaded. It was a noisy, colourful and lively place for the older Crighton boys to explore.

Robert returned to Scotland at least once more. He was with his son John Thomson Crighton when he died of tuberculosis aged only nineteen in February 1876 at 'Cornton Vale', Logie, Perthshire[198].

This was near the home of his Thomson grandparents, who were both buried in 1877; all are commemorated on a gravestone in Logie Churchyard, near Stirling[199].

Two of the surviving Crighton sons followed in their father's footsteps by becoming captains of merchant ships. Alexander started his apprenticeship in July 1876 aboard the *SS Ben Vorlich* of Glasgow and went on to become second mate (1881-2) on the *Pauline David* and the *Schaldis*, both brigs of Antwerp. Meanwhile 1877 saw the founding of Béliard Crighton, ship repairers and later, shipbuilders[200]. The Crighton part of the name refers to Robert's family and two of his grandsons became directors of the company. The same year, William started his four year apprenticeship on board *SS Mennock* of Liverpool, passing for second mate in 1881 (having twice failed his navigation exams) and proceeding to join various ships registered at Antwerp for short trips round the Mediterranean – until 1886, when he got his First Mate's and then his Master's Certificates[201].

Robert and Jane's daughter Jane married William Edward Dyke in Antwerp and their baby Mabel Jane was the only grandchild Robert ever saw. Unfortunately, she died aged only three months in early January, 1880 and ten days later Jane herself died aged about twenty-seven[202]. It must have been devastating to lose them both, especially so soon after John. There was a notice in the Deaths column of the *Liverpool Mercury*:

> *DYKE. Jan 14th at Rue Jordeans, Antwerp, Jennie, wife of W.E.Dyke, eldest daughter of Captain Crighton of Antwerp.*

The address suggests that the couple were living with Robert and Jane. Belgian certificates of the time do not give the cause of death but an infection such as tuberculosis is likely. There was a happier event later in the year when Robert junior married Mary Elizabeth Chapman at the British Embassy in Antwerp. Their eldest child, William Robert Crighton, was born at 51, Rue de Artevelde (Antwerp) on November 28th 1883.

Unfortunately this was too late for Robert. He died in the afternoon of November 27th, 1882, aged sixty-one, anecdotally of stomach cancer, and never knew he had a grandson. Alexander and William were both at sea and 'he was borne to his grave in a manner worthy of a brave sailor, on the shoulders of the quartermasters of the *Belgenland* and *Switzerland* with the Belgian, American and British flags covering as brave a heart as ever throbbed, followed by all the officers of the port in their uniforms'[203]. His burial place is unknown and any gravestone would probably have been destroyed by enemy action, if not previously removed to make way for other burials.

There were a few, rather brief obituaries in a few British newspapers, but others round the world were more fulsome. An Australian reporter wrote that Robert was 'better known and more honoured in America than in his native city of Liverpool' (!) and, 'it is pleasant to find that if few of his countrymen recollected the noble act of Captain Crighton, those to whom he displayed such brotherly feeling have all along shown better memories'[204].

The house at 91 Rue Jordeans remained the family home until July 1884, when Jane and Mary Catharine moved to Robert junior's house in Rue van Artevelde. After Mary's marriage to a wealthy stockbroker, George Symons, Jane went to live with them in England[205]. In 1908 the Rev Herbert Reid visited her for lunch in 'a London suburb', probably Monken Hadley, just off the Great North road, the home of the Symons family. He described Jane as 'a delightful old lady'. Coffee was served on the silver salver presented to Robert over fifty years before by the merchants of Boston. Intrigued by the words 'Be of good cheer, I will not desert you' engraved round the edge of the tray, Mr Reid learned about the rescue. On his return to the Port Glasgow area, he used the story to illustrate the talks he gave to children in Sunday school[206].

Jane died at Hadley Lodge at the grand old age of eighty-six and was buried in the local graveyard[207]. Sadly, the inscription gives no hint of Jane's adventurous life nor of her famous husband:

In Loving Memory of
JANE CRIGHTON
Born Sept 1st 1827
Died June 10th 1914

I will lay me down in peace and take my rest for it is thou
Lord only that makes me dwell in safety

Chapter Eleven
A Personal View of Robert

Robert was clearly a very skilful sailor by 1854 when he came across the wreck of the *San Francisco*. After nine years in command he had 'never been shipwrecked and the worst that has happened to him is the loss of nearly all his sails'. Shipwreck was a common occurrence in the mid-Nineteenth Century – it was estimated that a hundred and thirty US vessels alone were sunk in 1853[208] – and avoiding such a tragedy required great judgement and knowledge as well as good fortune.

Robert looks straight out of the 1854 etching, an extraordinarily good-looking man in the prime of life, full of confidence and in excellent health. One could reasonably ask if his features really were that perfect. His nose (unbroken) and his mouth (as far as one can tell under the moustache he later grew) seem the same in the later painted portrait and the one photograph that exists of him. In all three likenesses there are no traces of childhood illness or scars of any sort. He had grey eyes and a reddish tinge to his hair which eventually became quite white.

In an age where the average European was not much more than five-feet-five tall, at over six feet Robert was not only a metaphorical giant among men. Height as an adult is determined partly genetically and partly by environment. Poor nutrition, disease and pollution (such as lead from water pipes) can stunt growth and from Robert's height alone we know he was well-fed as a child and did not suffer from rickets. Three of his sons (Robert, Alexander and William) were also notably tall.

If a man is ever defined by a single act, then Robert's rescue of so many people in the face of overwhelming odds is such a deed.

His courage and selflessness on that occasion are beyond question but, among all the hyperbole written about him at the time, there is plenty to suggest that behind the steel was a modest man who genuinely believed that he had not done anything remarkable at all. This may be why, if the Bells kept the money collected for him (and I think they did), he made no fuss about it, at least publicly. Although frequently described as heroic or gallant – and without doubt he was both – there were plenty of other, quieter descriptors: generous, cordial, bluff, bashful, polite, big-hearted, self-sacrificing and full of the milk of human kindness.

Over the years of reading and thinking about Robert, I sense that one of his chief characteristics was friendliness. I see that in the etching of him and expressed in his letter to Stephen Massett, in the Reverend Wilson's diary and in his obituary in a local newspaper[209]:

In his young days Mr Crighton, just deceased, was a boon companion of the late ex-Bailie Livingston, Mr Davies, clothier and others of old Port Glasgow stock. [In Antwerp] he was frequently visited by many of his old friends.

Also, he was described as 'our friend Captain Crighton' in newspapers published as far apart as Jamaica and Australia.

It would be wonderful to have even one of the letters he and Jane must have written to each other in the years they were apart. The passengers on Robert's ships certainly liked and admired him, as witnessed by the diary and several letters in the press. His crews as well, in spite of the ban on spirits: 'No greater favourite with passengers or crew walks a ship's decks today'[210], although those dismissed for drunkenness might have been less enthusiastic. In an age where some merchant captains inflicted punishment so brutal that the men died or were maimed for life, he maintained discipline by other means. Mostly, I think, by example and force of character.

There are no physical punishments in any of the crew log books I have read.

It is difficult to believe there was no dark side but I have not found one. Perhaps one day there will be a small memorial to Captain Robert Crighton, of whom it can justly be said:

> *the elements*
> *So mixed in him that Nature might stand up*
> *And say to all the world, 'This was a man!'*
> (Shakespeare, *Julius Caesar*)

Part Two

Robert's Family

Chapter Twelve
Robert and Jane's Descendants

Although Robert and Jane had nine children, there are few descendants compared with his brother Alexander. Five of Jane's nine children died before her and three predeceased Robert. Only three of their children have known descendants, though it is possible that Alfred married again.

The children of Robert and Jane

Jane Crighton was born in Whampoa, China sometime between June 1852 and January 1853 and went to Antwerp with her family aged twenty-one. Her marriage and early death are described in Chapter 10.

Robert Crighton was born at Drumtogle farm, Auchterader, Perthshire on May 14th 1854, and married Mary Elizabeth Chapman in Antwerp. He was an apprentice engineer with the Britannia Engine Works in Birkenhead and worked for Heidel and Demblow before being employed by the Red Star Line in 1878[211]. In 1897 he bought a plot of land in Antwerp and had a beautiful Art Deco house built there, which still exists in its original form[212]. This house was sold in 1907 and the family returned to England where Robert was manager of Harland and Wolff's Southampton works before becoming Deputy Chairman of the company. His place on the maiden voyage of the *Titanic* in 1912 is said to have been taken over by 'a senior person', whose identity is unknown. Robert died suddenly in August 1924 and is commemorated with Mary on his mother's gravestone in Monken Hadley, though he may not be buried there.

Robert and Mary had seven children-

William Robert

Their eldest son, William volunteered in October 1917 while working for A. Bulcke & Co. in Antwerp and was posted to the Intelligence Corps[213]. He married (first) Stephanie Portielje and the couple's only child Robert had two step-daughters, one of whom has descendants. In 1941 William married Anna Lebornge and died in April 1943.

Arthur Edward Crighton

Another son, Arthur Edward Crighton, married and had a son, Richard, and a daughter, Elizabeth, always known as Betty. Richard married Barbara M. Page and has living descendants. He emigrated to Canada and wrote a magazine article about the loss of the *San Francisco* as well as two novels. Elizabeth wrote books under one of her married names, Betty James (e.g. *London for Lovers*, 1968). Her only child, Angus (Gus) Dudgeon (said to have 'discovered' Elton John) died without issue.

Gladys

A daughter, Gladys, married Edwin Gordon Boyd and they have living descendants.

John Thomson Crighton was born on February 7th, 1857, at sea when Jane accompanied Robert on the *Tornado*, and was christened in Bombay. Nothing further is known of him except that he died in Perthshire in 1876 aged only nineteen, of 'catarrhal pneumonia and acute phthisis, several months', in other words, tuberculosis.

Charles Edward Crighton was two years old on the 1861 census of Govan, born Auchterader, Perthshire. He died aged eight on Feb 5th 1867 and was buried in Flaybrick Memorial Garden in Birkenhead, which has been badly vandalised; there is no extant headstone.

Alexander Thomson Crighton was born on the 15th February 1861, at Govan and got his Master's Certificate in 1883. Six feet tall, with fair hair and blue eyes, he spent many years working on steamers of the Donaldson Line. While captain of their ship *Circe* he twice saved the lives of other sailors in 1889/90, the first time receiving an award from the United States Government:[214]

An interesting ceremony took place in the offices of the local Marine Board yesterday. Mr Nathaniel Dunlop, chairman, presented a gold watch and chain to Captain Crighton of the Donaldson Line steamer Circe, a gold medal and $50 to Mr Laing the mate and $25 each to (five named crewmen). The awards were made in recognition of services rendered to the crew of the American vessel Mary E. Dana on 17th March last. The Circe was 2 days sail from Baltimore when she came across the Mary E Dana lying waterlogged and the lives of the crew in danger. There was a heavy sea and the Circe stood to windward, spread oil on the waters, lowered a boat and allowed it to drift to leeward. The operation was twice repeated and by this means the captain and seven men were saved.

The inscription on the watch says it is from the President of the United States and Alex's surname is spelled Creighton. Less than a year later Alex again came to the aid of a helpless ship:

Halifax NS Feb 3*-Last evening the Donaldson Liner Circe, from Glasgow for Baltimore, arrived with the tank steamer Ocean in tow. The Ocean was from Rotterdam for New York. Captain Creighton of the Circe had experienced very heavy weather and lost his lifeboats. When 350 miles off Halifax he saw a steamer in the distance flying signals "starving" and "short of coal". He* *bore down on the helpless ship and found her to be the Ocean. Captain Voge said he had had a frightful voyage and was then 25 days out of Rotterdam. His coal was all gone and his crew were starving. He had previously obtained provisions from a passing ship but these were all gone and he requested Captain Creighton to take him in tow.*

A boat was launched but with some difficulty, involving nine hours' work. A line was got aboard the Ocean, but hardly had the Circe begun to tow when the five inch hawser parted.

It was then one hour after midnight and the breeze was so strong and the sea so high that nothing further could be done till daylight. Then another boat was launched, and after five hours of labor, two more steel hawsers were passed from the Ocean to the Circe. Before commencing to tow Captain Creighton sent a boat loaded with provisions on board the Ocean and on the afternoon of 30th proceeded to Halifax. All went well till Saturday night when one of the hawsers snapped, and the rest of the journey was made with one hawser. It took four days and two hours to tow the Ocean 350 miles[215].

There are some echoes here of the *San Francisco* rescue and Robert would surely have been very proud of his son.

Alex moved to Canada in 1894 and eventually became a Canadian citizen. In 1911 he was either living with or visiting his brother-in-law George Symons and sister Mary at Monken Hadley in Middlesex. He shot himself in the head in a sleeping carriage at St. Pancras on August 3rd, 1913[216]. His address was said to be Callander Hydro, Scotland and also a London club. The coroner's inquest records for that time have been destroyed but there may be a newspaper report. His estate was only was just over £100, which he left to his nephews Arthur and Charles. He did not marry.

William Bell Crighton was born on Jan 9th, 1863. He was half an inch short of six feet tall, with brown hair and blue eyes. After failing his navigation exams twice he became a master mariner in 1886 and commanded ships going to Australia. William died in June 1904 of complications from a ruptured appendix, aged forty-one. His brother Alexander was with him at the Seaman's Hospital, West Ham.

Lilian Clarissa and Kathleen (Belle?)
William married Annie Clarissa Flaherty and had two daughters, Lilian Clarissa and Kathleen (Belle?) Lilian was a trainee teacher in a girl's Catholic boarding school in Jersey in 1911 and Kathleen was a pupil at a similar school in Streatham near where the family lived. The girls visited their relatives in Antwerp together sometime in the early Twentieth Century[217]. Lilian died unmarried in 1970 and Kathleen probably in 1986.

Mary Catharine Crighton was born at Rock Ferry, Birkenhead in 1864. She married George Symons, a wealthy ship and stockbroker and they lived in Denmark Hill, London and afterwards at Monken Hadley, Barnet. George Symons died in 1917 and Mary Catharine in 1920, in Switzerland where she is buried.

Madeleine Jane Symons
Their only child, Madeleine Jane Symons, graduated from Newnham College, Cambridge, in 1916. This was in the middle of World War 1 when women were doing work formerly done by men, often for very low wages. Madeleine joined the staff of the National Federation of Women Workers, founded by Mary Macarthur in 1906. As head of the Negotiations Department she became famed as an orator in arbitration cases that she won eighty per cent of the time[218]. After the war she helped to negotiate unemployment pay for the women thrown out of work by returning servicemen. She sat

on many committees including the Royal Commission for Lunacy and was in demand as a member of trade boards. For many years she was the senior chairman of the West London Juvenile Court and advocated raising the age of criminal responsibility, arguing that young offenders were more in need of care and protection than of punishment. Madeleine looked after the orphaned daughter of Mary Macarthur after the latter's early death in 1921[219]. In the 1920s she was romantically involved with Dr J.J. Mallon, a man whose life was 'devoted to social amelioration'[220]. The couple had one natural and one adopted child.

In 1940 Madeleine married Professor Harold R. Robinson, F.R.S., who had worked with Lord Rutherford on atomic structure. Harold died in 1955 and Madeleine in 1957.

Terence Richard and Teresa Mary Symons
Terence Richard Symons was killed on active service 21st February 1945 aged only twenty. Teresa married and had two children, dying in 1972.

Alfred James Crighton was born at Rock Ferry in the March quarter of 1868. He was a boarder at the Dollar Academy in Clackmannanshire 1881-1883, where he gained prizes in Mathematics, Latin, French and German[221]. He married Agnes Ritchie in Edinburgh in 1888 and was seventh engineer on a ship bound for Australia in 1890. On census night 1891 they were living in Lanarkshire but went to live in Antwerp in 1898. Eight years later Agnes reported her change of address to the Belgian authorities, having separated from her husband-who was paying her three hundred francs a month in alimony[222]. They had no children and so far no further trace has been found of Alfred.

Norman Septimus Crighton was born on March 16th 1871 in Victoria Road, Upper Bebington, Wirral. He died of whooping cough on September 28th that year.

Chapter Thirteen

Alexander and Margaret, Robert's Brother and Sister

Alexander

Alexander McKeich Crighton was named for his maternal grandfather, Alexander Lang; McKeich was his mother Jeannie's maiden name. He began his sea-going apprenticeship on the *Marion* in 1838, just after his sixteenth birthday and two years later 'got my arm broke'[223]. On census night 1841 he was living with his grandmother Margaret McKeich at King Street, probably convalescing from his fractured arm. He returned to the sea in December 1841 and sailed as an ordinary (or perhaps able) seaman for nearly two years and then as second mate on the *Rebecca* of Greenock. On the Certificate of Service accompanying the application for his mate's certificate, Alexander wrote 'Sept 1843 Wrecked off King's Island'. The *Rebecca* was on her way from London to Sydney and left Batavia on August 19th. On September 19th they encountered a hurricane and 'for 14 hours she lay beamed' (with the deck perpendicular to the sea, extremely uncomfortable and dangerous)[224]. It was six days before her captain made a reliable land sighting: the north coast of King Island in the Bass Strait. King Island is in the Roaring Forties, about half way between Tasmania and Australia, its rocky north-west corner the site of many shipwrecks.

The *Rebecca's* anchors were dropped because it was getting dark. In the morning the ship was surrounded by rocky reefs, but it was very difficult to see them for thick blankets of kelp. A whaleboat with 'an old man', Mr Scott, and his family of two adult women, a boy of about twelve and three girls came alongside. They needed nails and other supplies and confirmed that the narrow channel by which the *Rebecca* had sailed through the reefs was the only way back to the open sea. The whaleboat left for the shore but overturned in the surf and old Scott and the youngest girl were drowned. One woman took the boy and the other held on to both surviving girls and these five somehow made it to safety.

A south-westerly wind was essential to get through the narrow channel but it was two days before one blew up and then it was gale force. Both anchors had to be cut free because there was no time for them to be weighed (wound up). Then the wind turned, blowing the ship back to the shore. Tacking did not take them any further away and the breakers were getting ever nearer. Cables and the remaining anchors could not delay the inevitable and 'there was every indication of a tempest', so the longboat was lowered and the *Rebecca's* sick passengers, plus a woman and twelve of the crew, got in. They reached safety but the longboat had been badly damaged. The smaller quarter boat was lowered into the rough sea but the men who got aboard first let the painter (holding rope) go slack and it was swamped under the lee side of the ship. One of the carpenters, the steward and a seaman were drowned. Having no other way to save himself and the rest of the crew, the first mate set the helm to drive the *Rebecca* straight onto the land. The surf threw the ship further up the shore and she did not break up as she would have done if beached broadside on. The captain must have been in the longboat, though he did not admit this in his report.

That night there was another storm. Only a handful of seal or wallaby hunters and their families lived on the island, so food, shelter and dry clothes were probably unobtainable. The next day repairs to the longboat began and some of the crew were ordered to collect what could be salvaged from the *Rebecca*. They swam through the surf and sent bundles down a wire from ship to shore. The captain left his brother-in-law and four men guarding the ship and set off with twelve hands to row to Williamstown (near Melbourne) on October 14th. After two days they had to return to repair the longboat again and finally reached Williamstown a week later. Here some of the crew demanded their wages and found themselves locked up in the Watch House, accused by the captain of drunkenness, insubordination and robbery. The charges could not be substantiated and the case was dismissed.

Although Alexander was definitely on the *Rebecca*, he is not named in the newspaper reports of the wreck and apparently did not work on a ship again until July 1846. In 1849/50 he returned to Australia as second mate on the *Zarah* under Robert as captain. Afterwards there was another gap until October 1852, when he was second mate on the *John Bartlet* of London for seven months. He was then awarded his First Mate's Certificate, giving the King Street address.

He did not get a UK Master's Certificate but continued with his sea-going career and was wrecked again on Cuba, date and ship unknown. Taken to Jamaica for a passage back to Scotland, he met James Goodchild Coe junior who had been the Chief Magistrate (Governor) of the Cayman Islands, then a Jamaican dependency. James owned a schooner and persuaded Alexander to accompany him to Grand Cayman, where he lived with his family including two unmarried daughters. Apparently one of their brothers saw his father returning with a young(ish) man and told his sisters an eligible bachelor was arriving. The elder girl (whom James was particularly keen to have off his hands!) said she was never going to marry a man she did not know but the younger one, Ann, rose to the challenge[225]. Their eldest son, Alexander, was born in 1863.

Alexander and Ann settled at Spotts, a beautiful part of Grand Cayman, where they lived for the rest of their lives. Their homestead had two hundred yards of beach frontage, which must have been wonderful for their six children if there was ever time for playing. Among the food staples were cassava, breadfruit and yams. Mangoes grew everywhere and the beaches provided shellfish similar to hermit crabs as well as turtles in season. Venomous snakes were unknown, the crocodiles (from which the Islands got their name, 'caimans') had been hunted to extinction and the only indigenous mammals were bats. However, there were (and are) some very poisonous plants, particularly the machineel tree, the fruits of which were called 'little death apples' by Christopher Columbus. It is one of the top-ten most dangerous plants in the world, with caustic sap. Vast numbers of mosquitoes inhabited the central swamps but, thankfully, malaria and dengue fever have never been endemic on the islands and there were very few cases before 1912.

Some or all of the four sons of the family were also sea captains. They and a son-in-law had homesteads next to one another where cattle were raised. One time they imported a fine bull and two cows from America to improve the stock. They did their own butchery, tanned the leather and employed a Jamaican to make shoes from it. The family owned a six-foot-wide dug-out canoe called 'Port Glasgow' which needed several men to row but was useful for ferrying supplies like flour and kerosene. Alexander and Ann also had two daughters, one of whom did not marry. Unlike Robert's side of the family, they have many, many descendants.

Alexander continued to captain schooners for a while, sailing up the eastern coast of America as far as Boston. However, he had a much-needed skill and when he retired from the sea he opened a school of navigation[226]:

> *Alexander Mckeith Crighton was a valuable immigrant in that he had a thorough knowledge of navigation and was willing to impart it to others. We have related in the past how precarious navigation was and that, with the exception of Richard Phelan nobody really understood the art. Crighton trained and taught others and carried on the work begun by Phelan.*

He eventually became a storekeeper like his father and died aged seventy-one on February 24th 1894, from a gunshot wound thought to be sustained while shooting rabbits. A coroner's inquest was held the same day but the death certificate records only 'shot in the head by a gun' without any further verdict[227]. Presumably foul play was not suspected. He died at 'Spotts, Prospect' which would have been on or near the beach and is buried at Spotts Cemetery close to his wife Ann, who died in 1899. Their gravestones have the Crighton spelling.

There never have been any rabbits on the Cayman Islands, but agoutis (a kind of rodent) were introduced by the early settlers[228] and are apparently very good to eat. Although their meat was prized, turtles are out at sea in February and they were netted or trapped rather then shot.

There is a family story that Alexander made a down-payment on some land in the area that became downtown Chicago, arranging to pay the remainder and take title at a later date[229]. Unfortunately his paperwork was lost in a shipwreck and the corresponding proof in Chicago was destroyed by fire, so the deal could not be completed.

At first sight this seems rather far-fetched, but Alexander did go to Chicago when he was an apprentice on the *Marion*. She left Greenock on July 4th 1839 carrying emigrants for the Argyle settlement in Illinois and reached Chicago fifty-three days later[230]. Here plots of land were being sold by the Receiver of Public Monies, but how could Alexander – who was not yet seventeen – have put down a deposit? Apprentices, if they were paid at all, received about one shilling (5p) a month. He had probably worked in the family shop before going to sea and perhaps got lucky at cards in Chicago's saloons or on the racetrack, of which there were several on the edge of town by 1830[231].

The fractured arm meant that Alexander did not finish his apprenticeship and was not employed at sea from January until December 1841. Then he served as an ordinary seaman on two ships before joining the ill-fated *Rebecca*. After she was wrecked in late 1843 he landed in Australia, probably with little more than the clothes he was wearing. Any documents he owned would have been completely destroyed by water.

Alexander must have returned to Britain by ship, but did not work on one for more than two years[232], until he joined the *Foam* at Liverpool in July 1846. During this time he could have accumulated enough money to complete the purchase and travel to Chicago. The first payable gold was not mined in Australia until 1851 but gambling thrived around cricket and horseracing well before then[233]. He was due some wages and maybe fortune smiled on him again.

The duplicate papers in Chicago could well have been burned. Nineteen buildings were destroyed by fire in October 1839 and there were two major blazes in 1841, consuming first five houses and later about a dozen more. These included the County Clerk's office, though the books and papers were said to have been saved. The *Chicago American* commented (rather presciently) that 'our city appears to be doomed in the way of fire'. [234] Nothing in the story can be proved, except that Alexander was at Chicago in 1839 when parcels of land were being sold and had time enough to return after the wreck of the *Rebecca*. It is unlikely that the shipwreck concerned was the later one off Cuba with the proof being lost in the Great Fire of 1871, because downtown Chicago was already developed by then.

Margaret

Robert's sister Margaret married James Thomson in June, 1847, only five months after her mother died. At first they lived in the family house at King Street with their children, Jeanie, John and Margaret (Maggie), which provided a base for Robert and Alexander when they were not at sea. Then James's job took him first to Aberdeen where another son (James) was born, and on to Edinburgh. Here, after a gap of nearly nine years their last child, Robert Alexander, arrived[235].

In 1871 Margaret sold the house in Port Glasgow that her mother had officially sold but had probably given to her (Chapter 15). She needed her husband's permission to do so even though the house was hers. As a safeguard, she had to appear in front of the lawyers without him to affirm that no pressure had been put on her to sell[236].

By 1891 Margaret was a widow, supporting herself and her daughter Maggie by keeping apartments in Edinburgh. Maggie died in 1900 (the cause on her death certificate, 'neurasthenia', is not a precise diagnosis. Paralysis is mentioned). Robert, a machinery agent, then moved back to live with his mother until she died aged 77 in 1903, of senile debility. He never married and died a few days after World War Two was declared in 1939 aged 76, of 'acute cardio dilatation' (!) This was at ten minutes past midnight at the home of his 'intimate friend' Mary (surname illegible) – rather an extraordinary entry on a death certificate in mid-twentieth century Edinburgh.

Margaret and James's eldest daughter Jeanie (full name Jane Crighton Thomson) married William Robertson, a General Merchant, at Leith in 1874. They had two children in Edinburgh, Margaret J.T.C. (? Jane Thomson Crighton) Robertson and William, aged 5 and 2 in 1881. The family then disappear from the Scottish records. In the 1991 and 1901 censuses for Knowsley, Lancashire there is a couple who could be Jane and William, with a daughter Jeannie, all born in Scotland, but there is no sign of Margaret or William junior.

Nothing more has been found of Margaret and James's other children John and James[237].

Chapter Fourteen

Robert's Crighton Ancestors

It sometimes seemed as though the origins of the Crighton family would never be found, there were so many false leads and dead ends. Robert was born in 1821 to another Robert, grocer of Port Glasgow, but finding his Crighton grandparents took a great deal of detective work.

The Parish Registers of Port Glasgow[238] and surrounding area contain only two possible baptisms for Robert senior:

Greenock New or Middle
1780 Robert lawfull son to William Crighton blacksmith and Elizabeth Ross his spouse born 26th and baptised 27th May.
Other sons were called John and Peter.

This baptism looked like a promising starting place but there is no proof that it is right one. Suggestive it might not be is the fact that Robert senior did not use the names John, Peter, William or Elizabeth for his children. There was a very strong naming tradition in Scotland and northern England: the first son was usually given his paternal grandfather's name, the next his maternal grandfather's and the third his father's. It is not possible to discover if this baby, Robert, born 1780, survived to adulthood because there are no useful apprenticeship or burial records. It is always good to check this detail. All too frequently children who actually died as infants appear on family trees with a wife and several children.

The other possible baptism is:

Port Glasgow
06/09/1774 Robert, son of James Creighton carpenter and
Elizabeth Ker
Other children were Margaret, James and Elizabeth.

This family then disappeared from the Port Glasgow records –
there are no further parish register entries after Elizabeth's birth in
1779. If this is the right Robert, he would have been forty-four when
he married Jeannie, but, again, Robert senior did not call his eldest
son James which makes this baptism slightly less likely.

Neither James Creighton, carpenter, nor William Crighton,
blacksmith, left a will. Had they done so one of these men might have
been confirmed as Robert senior's father, or both been eliminated.

Knowledge of Robert senior's age at death in 1828 would also
have been useful in determining which, if either, of these baptisms
was likely to be his. There are no burial records of the time, no age was
given in the death notice in the *Glasgow Herald* and no gravestone
survives, if there ever was one. Another closed door.

The parish records show that Jeannie was not Robert's first wife:

Port Glasgow
June 2nd 1811 Robert Creichton Grocer in Port Glasgow and
Isabella Colquhoun residing there were booked in order to
proclamation for marriage

This date provides some indication of a birth year. Subtracting
sixteen (the earliest usual age to marry) from 1811 gives 1795 as the
latest year he is likely to have been born. He was probably older than
sixteen when he married as the description of 'grocer' seems rather
too established for a man in his mid-teens.

Robert senior's will was quite surprising. When proved at Paisley
in 1830, there was an inventory of the shop's stock, his household

goods and all the debts. These were mostly small amounts owed on monthly account by trusted customers, but:

Item 3. Principal Sum contained in a Discharge and Renunciation by Mrs Elizabeth Semple Relict of the deceased John Dunlop Esq. Merchant in Port Glasgow in favour of the representatives of the deceased Adam Crighton sailmaker there dated 7th May 1824 – £300 Interest at 5% £22.10

Item 4. Debts due to the deceased by Current Account of the foresaid Adam Crighton of which it is thought not more than one pound can be recovered £344.16

£666.26 was a huge debt. It was more than the combined value of Robert's stock in the shop, cash at hand and at the bank, and his household goods. It would have bought two ordinary houses or a mansion. Unusually (and unfortunately) no relationship between Adam and Robert was given in the will, though the amount involved suggested a close family tie. The parish registers for the whole of Scotland were searched for a suitable Robert Crighton related to an Adam, without success. There was an Adam Crighton having children in Port Glasgow in the early Nineteenth Century but there did not seem to be any connection to a Robert. The Mitchell Library at the University of Glasgow could not help with the 'Discharge and Renunciation' of 1824. Another dead end, apparently.

Were there any other sources of information about this family? In 1910, the Governor of the Cayman Islands wrote a history of the place including as much as he could discover of the genealogy of the early settlers[239]:

Robert Crighton was born at Port Glasgow and was a surgeon

in Jamaica where he died. His son James lived in Scotland and
had a son Robert who died in 1826 in Antwerp.
Robert had five sons, the third one of whom Alexander McKeith
was born in Glasgow in 1822.

Although confused and inaccurate, this was worth investigating.

The only Robert Crighton who had a father called James born about the right time was the one already found, 1774. This James (a carpenter) was married in Port Glasgow and, very interestingly, had another son Adam in 1784; by then the family had moved to Lanarkshire. James went to sea and must have done well (prize money?) or perhaps his wife inherited some wealth because they bought a property in Hamilton, Lanarkshire[240]. Their grave is inscribed:[241]

Here lies the remains of James Creighton esquire of Greenfield
who died 18th January 1789 aged 43 years.
The sky his canopy the earth his bed
Who braved the seas he's numbered with the dead.
Also the remains of Elizabeth Kerr his spouse who died 26th
January 1822 aged 72 years. She was an affectionate wife, a
tender mother and a faithful friend.

'Esquire' is quite a step up from carpentry. It seemed this was the right family, because information from two independent sources fitted together. Here was a Robert Crighton with a father called James (a 'fact' from the Cayman Islands book) and a brother Adam (for the debt mentioned in Robert's will).

This Robert Crighton, a merchant, married Rosina Trotter in Dunbartonshire in 1803 and had a son, James, in Glasgow (1804). Rosina and baby James do not appear in any other records, the couple had no further children and there are no burial records to discover what happened to them. When Robert sold the Lanarkshire property in 1804[242], he was not described as 'of Port Glasgow' but 'of Berensfield' (part of Hamilton). Nevertheless, the facts could be made to fit: Rosina and James probably died soon after the baby's birth, Robert sold the property and used the proceeds to set up a grocery business in Port Glasgow between 1804 and 1811 when he married Isabella. Proof was lacking but it was a working hypothesis.

Was there any confirmation of the other statement in the book on the Cayman Islands: that James's father Robert was a surgeon in Jamaica? Many Scots left for the Caribbean after the 1745 Jacobite Rising and some became wealthy plantation owners. They preferred their own doctors and book-keepers who emigrated to work for them. From his gravestone we know James was born about 1746, but not where. There is no suitable baptism in the Port Glasgow parish register.

There *was* a Dr Robert Crighton in the parish of St. Ann, Jamaica who was taxed on his slaves and cattle in 1792 but not afterwards – he had probably died[243]. It is quite possible for this man to have been the father of James Creighton of Hamilton (born *circa* 1746), if James returned to Port Glasgow some time before he married. This was promising but there is no evidence of a connection between these two men and there are no records of a burial, a will or headstone to provide any.

It looked as though every available avenue had been researched as far as possible without Robert senior's origins being found. However, there was one last clue to follow up. Captain Robert's obituary in the *Greenock Telegraph* (Chapter 10) says that his parents *owned* the shop in King Street, known as 'Crighton's Land'. This was unusual enough for the reporter to comment on it because, at the time, most people rented their homes and business accommodation. Full details of property sales were written into the Registers of Sasines and have been preserved. A sasine (rhymes with 'raisin') is the granting of the legal right to feudal property. The transfer of ownership was symbolized by handing over earth and stone, with grass and corn if farmland. Vendors of property had to prove they owned what they were selling – and if ownership was by inheritance, their ancestors were named.

When Captain Robert claimed his father's share of the King Street in 1847[244], he produced in court the documents that proved his right to:

> *the just and equal one-fifth part... of that piece of ground... in Port Glasgow... subscribed by Mrs Elizabeth Semple from whom the same was purchased* **by Adam Crighton, Grandfather of the said Robert Crighton.**

So Adam was actually Robert senior's *father*! And this information fits exactly with the latter's will, even including Mrs Elizabeth Semple. The details about the family in the book on the Cayman Islands are mostly mistaken, though the Christian names alone suggest that the Creightons of Hamilton could have a common origin with the Crightons of Port Glasgow. With this new fact a lot more could be discovered about the family from parish registers.

Baptisms, father Adam Crighton, mother Janet Shaw:

Greenock Old or West
John 04/11/1787
Greenock New or Middle
Janet 06/09/1789
Agnes 22/01/1792

Port Glasgow
William 8/11/1795

Helen 7/12/1800
Adam 09/06/1805

And a marriage:

Greenock New or Middle Church.
December 1ˢᵗ 1786 Adam Creighton, Sailmaker and Janet Shaw
daughter of William Shaw farmer in Inverkip

John and Helen must have died young because there is no further mention of them. Adam clearly moved from Greenock to Port Glasgow and was a sailmaker, which tallies with Robert senior's will.

Robert's name is not among these baptisms, but there is a twenty-two month gap between the births of John and Janet, which is enough time for another child and fits with Robert being born prior to 1795. There is evidence for this: Adam senior did not leave a will but, in 1822, he settled his property on his five children, named as Robert, Janet, Agnes, William and Adam. The children other than Robert are listed in birth order, so Robert was probably older than Janet. Also, in the 1824 Discharge and Renunciation document (when it was finally found in the Scottish National Archives) recording Robert senior's payment of the whole amount due on the house, he is described as the '*eldest* son and representative of the deceased Adam Crighton'

Since it is very unlikely he was not baptised at all, what might account for the lack of a record?

Adam's first son John was christened in the Old, West Church and Janet and Agnes in the New, Middle Church. The Minister of the Old Kirk, Allan McAulay, was appointed in 1786, but soon there were 'alleged improprieties of behaviour.' His case was heard in the Town Hall but McAulay died before it could be concluded[245]. Unfortunately the Kirk Session Records (equivalent of vestry minutes, the record of church affairs) of the time are lost – they were kept in the Manse and the late Minister's wife never returned them. They would have made entertaining reading (and might also have had some information about Adam). In his history of Greenock, Daniel Weir says of this period that 'the register of births cannot but be inaccurate from the negligence of parents on this important point'. The negligence may have been in the recording as well as in the ceremonies themselves: the parish register lists baptisms in date order on the right-hand pages but some otherwise blank left-hand pages have up to four more apparently written in some time after the events. It seems that the Minister may have forgotten to make up his books on occasion and (sometimes) made good the omission later.

Or it could be that Robert was baptised privately because he was sickly. Such a baby would generally be welcomed into the Kirk publicly some time later, when the details of both ceremonies would be recorded in the parish register. In the move to the New Kirk, perhaps the second baptism was forgotten. Whatever the reason, Robert was probably born about 1788, the eldest surviving child of Adam Crighton and Janet Shaw. It is unusual that he did not call his eldest son Adam after his father or use any Crighton Christian names except his own.

It is possible to find earlier members of the Crighton family. Adam died between signing his settlement in May 1822 and July 1823 when Robert senior went to court to 'seise' the property. Adam's age at death is not known, but a limit can be put on his birth date by his marriage in 1786. Sailmaker's apprenticeships were for seven years from the age of fourteen, during which time the young man could not marry[246]. Subtracting seven plus fourteen from 1786 gives the latest year in which he could have been born as 1765.

These are the Crighton entries in the two Greenock churches:

Baptisms
All New or Middle Kirk

1742	*Creighton Alexander*	*Alexander Creighton and Margaret Rae*
1745	**Crichton John**	**Robert Crichton Agnes Mill**
		(Robert's occupation, ship master)
1748	*Crichtoun Margaret*	*Robert Crichton Margaret Millar*
1749	**Crichtoun Adam**	**Robert Crichtoun Agnes Mills**
1750	*Crichton Robert*	*John Crichton Ann Walker*
1750	*Crichton Phillip*	*John Crichton Ann Walker*
1750	*Crichtoun Josiah*	*Robert Crichtoun Margaret Millar*
1752	*Creighton Agnes*	*Robert Creighton Agnes Mills*
1754	*Creighton Eleanora*	*Robert Creighton Agnes Mills*
1754	*Crichton Walter*	*John Crichton and Ann Walker*
		(Old or West Kirk)
1756	*Crichton Edward*	*Robert Crichton Ann McLerran*

Clearly, there were two Robert Crightons in Greenock 1745-1754 and one probably had a brother called John. There are no baptism or marriage records for anyone called Crighton (or variations of the name) in Greenock during the 1760s.

Marriages

1737 (Old or West)	*Crichtoun Alexander*	*Margaret Rae*
1748 (New or Middle)	*Crichtoun John*	*Ann Walker*
1755	*Crichton Robert*	*Ann McLerran*

If the Adam Crighton, baptised in 1749, is the right person, he was thirty-seven when he married Janet Shaw. This is quite old for a first marriage but no other has been found (and Scottish parish register entries do not distinguish between bachelors and widowers). There is another possibility[247], but the most likely parents for Adam

Crighton, sail maker, are Robert Crighton (shipmaster of Greenock) and Agnes Mills.

There are a few earlier, tantalising Crighton records in Greenock:

Greenock Old or West,
Baptisms

15/06/1721 Helen   *Robert Crichton*   *Agnes McLirie*
06/07/1729 Mary   *Robert Crichton*   *Agnes McLeiry*
Robert's occupation, sailor

And two early burial records
26/11/1723 Helen d Rob Crishton (presumably the baby, above)
23/11/1732 Helen d Robert Crighton (if not, then this one probably is)

It is tempting to suggest that this Robert was the father of Robert Crighton who married Agnes Mills and he probably is the earliest member of the correct family that can be found. There are extant Hearth Tax (1691) and Poll Tax (1695) records for Renfrewshire, but no Crighton (or variants) appear. Almost all the inhabitants of Greenock were fishermen then and were probably too poor to pay the six shillings per hearth.

Adam's wife Janet Shaw was baptised on 26th December 1762 in Inverkip, parents William Shaw (farmer) and Agness Carswell. Her mother may be the Agnes Creswall baptised to James and Margaret Barr or Morrison on 9th September 1737 in Inverkip. Shaw was a common (and important) name in the area and no definite baptism can be found for William.

There is a very interesting entry in the Session Minutes of the Greenock West Kirk[248]:

April 23rd 1793

The Session, considering the state of the poor's box, were unanimously of the opinion that Mr William Shaw, their present treasurer, had not kept regular books during the time of his being in office and their opinion is founded on his own confession that he had burned the original books and that it was only a [illegible word] copy of them that he had laid before the Session. The Session unanimously agreed to suspend Mr Shaw from his office.

This scandal would have brought considerable shame on the family of the culprit. If he was Janet's father, this might have been the reason for the Crighton family's move to Port Glasgow between the births of Agnes in 1792 and William in 1795. However, there were three men called William Shaw living in the Greenock area at the time and no evidence to suggest which one was the thief.

Robert Crighton *m* Agnes Mills

John
1745

Adam Crighton *m* Janet Shaw
1749   1762

Janet
1789

Agnes
1792

William
1795

Helen
1800

Adam
1805

John
1787

Robert *m* Jeannie McKeich
c 1788   1798

Robert Crighton *m* Jane Thomson
1821   1827

Alexander McKeich
1822

Margaret Lang
1825

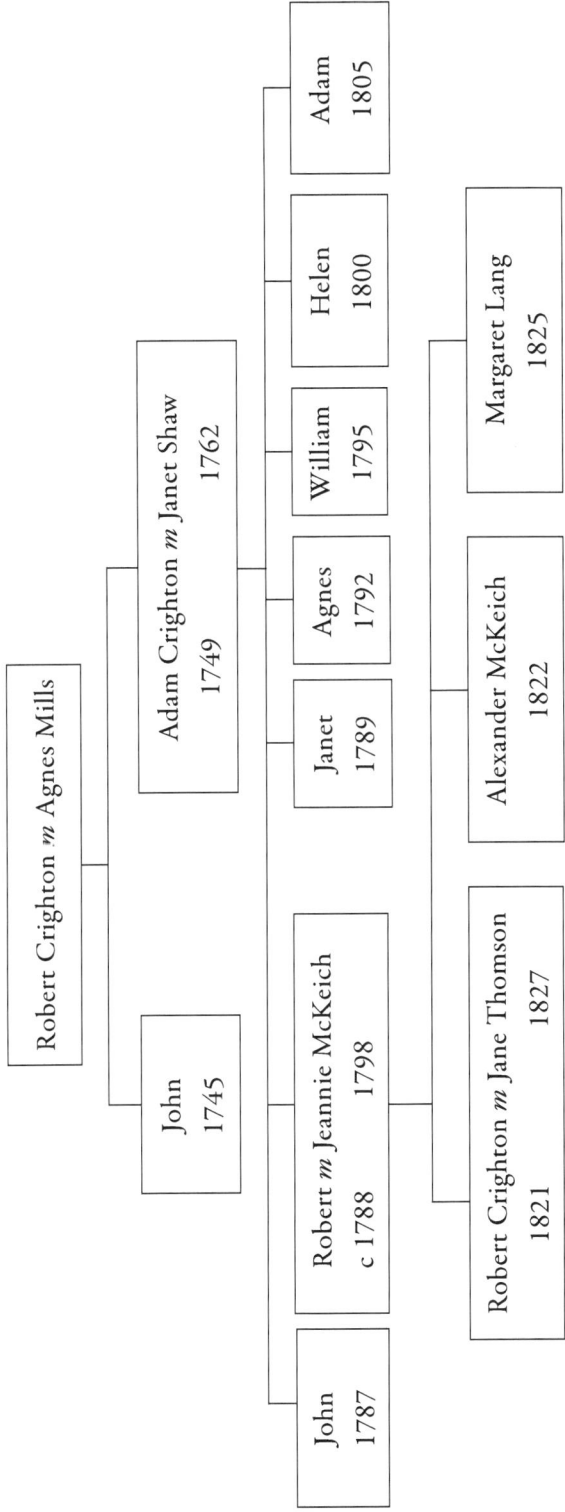

Simplified family tree of the Crightons. All dates are baptisms.

Chapter Fifteen
Adam, Robert and Jeannie

A family tree is only the beginning. The real interest lies in trying to discover more about our ancestor's lives than just when they were born, married, had children and died. If only we could go back to the early Nineteenth Century, just for a day, to see for ourselves what life was like in Port Glasgow or to the mid-Eighteenth Century in Greenock, where Adam was born. Documents and published histories have to substitute for this impossibility and from them a kind of fuzzy snapshot emerges.

Greenock does not seem to have been a particularly pleasant or safe place when Adam lived there[249]. The fresh water supply was never sufficient to meet the demand and the sewage ran in open drains. The streets were unpaved and unlit and there was no night watch to prevent brawling. Epidemics of smallpox and other fevers raged intermittently. On the plus side, there was plenty of work and the town had a grammar school from 1727. By 1810 there were twenty-three other schools, though even primary education was not then compulsory.

Settlements on the banks of the River Clyde, including Greenock, were all originally founded on the herring industry. The supply seemed inexhaustible. On one night in 1787, the fish were so closely packed together it was difficult for the boats catching them to move. By the early years of the Seventeenth Century, there was also employment in the shipbuilding industry and 1725 (when the population of Greenock was about one thousand) saw the beginning of rope and sailcloth manufacture. The town grew in importance as the number of trading vessels in the Clyde increased but facilities lagged behind. Until 1763 there was no flesh market or slaughterhouse. Farmers brought their cattle to town to sell to the butchers who killed and cut them up on the streets and sold the meat on the spot. The mess, stench and flies must have been appalling, but when a covered market was built the butchers had to be ordered to use it. Some years later there were still no assizes, and bakers could make bread of whatever size and ingredients they pleased with impunity. There was a shortage of meal and in 1785 a riot erupted, mostly of starving women whose families were in great need. The church stepped in, buying corn and selling it cheaply, but only on two days a week and in limited amounts. In 1800, a market for eggs, poultry, fish and garden produce opened but that was too late for the Crighton family to patronise.

There was a plentiful supply of cheap fish (subsidised by the town council), but the shortage of fresh water was always a serious problem, especially for shipmasters who found it difficult to replenish their barrels. The ten sugar refineries and other industries such as sailcloth making used a great deal of the limited water available. Even after a water company was set up in 1825 there was never enough. Politically the town was very advanced. Every proprietor of land had a vote in the election of the magistrates who had to seek a mandate for many of their actions, and the public accounts were open to inspection. This seemed to be sufficient democracy for the citizens of Greenock, because no-one could be found to speak for the Chartists when they sought universal male suffrage and other, equally valid, objectives from 1839 to 1848.

Sails were vital for as long as ships were powered by wind and there was always employment for those who made or repaired them. Adam would have served a seven year sailmaking apprenticeship, which he had to complete or risk imprisonment. Apprentices could be sued for damages if they did not conduct themselves 'decently and honestly', and anything they earned belonged to their master, even if it was prize money. An apprentice could not marry without his master's permission and was generally expected to behave in a sober fashion, though they seldom had the means to do anything else[250].

Physical strength was needed to make sails. A bolt of 'duck' (linen or hemp) was thirty-eight yards (about thirty-five metres) long, two feet (sixty centimetres) wide and weighed up to forty-four pounds (twenty kilos)[251].The mainsail of a square-rigged ship could need up to a *thousand yards* of duck and a complete set of sails would need ten times that amount. Large, foreign-going vessels might carry three complete sets of sails with spare duck and a sailmaker to repair or replace them. It was also his duty to sew the bodies of those who had died into odd pieces of canvas (with weights) for burial at sea.

Pictures of the large lofts in which sails were made show men sitting at narrow benches, from which hung leather tool bags. Lengths of duck were cut and then seamed together with double flat seams, sometimes in a curved fashion. The sewing twine was run through a block of beeswax or dipped in oil to soften it and three lengths were used together in the needle. There were usually 108-116 stitches per yard (just under a metre). Rope was then sewn round the edges of the sail to which handmade grommets were attached for the rigging. After soaking in sea water to prevent mildew, the sails were sometimes coloured with ochre and then rubbed with horse grease or linseed oil to repel water.

There are no Crightons listed among the sail makers in John Tait's *Directory of Glasgow* of 1784, but there is a Matthew Orr in Greenock. Another man of nearly that name, Mathew Orr (born Greenock 1793, father Joseph) invented the angulated jib where the cloth was cut at an angle across rather than parallel to the vertical warp threads, making the sail stronger[252]. He also developed a method for calculating the cutting and preparation of sails which did not require the whole sail to be laid out, saving both time and space. In addition, he improved the strength of the cloth considerably by doubling the number of warp threads. Mathew Orr also promoted the use of Irish, rather than Russian, linen, which was good news for the Irish flax growers, among them the ancestors of the Boyd family – see this book's dedication.

Adam married Janet Shaw on December 1st, 1786. Four children – John, Robert, Janet and Agnes – were born in Greenock but John must have died young because there are no further records of him. Sometime after the birth of Agnes in 1792 the family moved to Port Glasgow, where William was born in 1795. The move could have been to improve Adam's employment prospects or to ensure his children's education, because Greenock had no (free) parochial schools in the forty years up to 1809[253]. A Rope and Duck Company begun in Port Glasgow in 1736 was sold to The Gourock Ropework Company in 1774, which then moved all their operations to Port Glasgow. Somewhat confusingly the Gourock name was retained though the company was also known as the 'Birkmyre Ropeworks' after the owners. They manufactured sails as well as ropes, sailcloth and cordage and employed many people. Adam may have been among them; he seems never to have owned his own business.

It is difficult to believe now, but once there was thick woodland between Greenock and the Port and only a narrow track connected the two places, which was widened and stones put down a few years before the Crighton family moved. In Port Glasgow, tradesmen's houses of the time were only sixteen or seventeen feet square (about five metres by five), built of local stone and roofed with turf and straw. There was plenty of work for men like Adam. In 1775, over eleven thousand tons of shipping were employed in the foreign trade (timber, tobacco, brandy and wine, salt), 692 in the coastal trade and 795 of the herring fleet, and all of those ships needed sails[254].

Another girl, Helen, was born to Adam and Janet in 1800 but also died young. Adam, (born 1805) was disabled in some way, because in 1822 his father wrote that he was 'unable to earn a livelihood to himself'. Janet was forty-three when he was born which makes Down's syndrome a possibility. Secondary education was the preserve of the wealthy and Robert would have started work as soon as he was old enough. He was already a grocer (suggesting he had his own business) when he married

Isabella Colquhoun in 1811.Two girls of that name were baptised in Dunbartonshire in the 1790s, at Cardross, across the river from Port Glasgow but there is no evidence to suggest which one married Robert.

In 1811 a great comet appeared in the sky over Scotland. It inspired the name of the first steam-propelled ship to be built in Scotland, at John Wood's shipyard in Port Glasgow. Henry Bell, an inn-keeper at Helensburgh, wanted to advertise his business so he commissioned one of the new ships he had heard about to draw attention to his hotel and to bring customers from Glasgow[255]. On the day the *Comet* first sailed up the Clyde with a piper playing in the bow, many, many people, surely including some of the Crightons, 'flocked to jeer but stayed to marvel'[256].

On September 6th 1820, at the age of seventy-one, or perhaps only in his fifties, Adam bought a house on the corner of King Street and Lyon's Lane[257]. It cost £300, which he did not have. The vendor, Mrs E. Semple, granted him a loan of the full amount with the property as security[258]. There was a heavy penalty of sixty pounds for not repaying the debt in the agreed time, which was only fourteen months from the date of the sale. Interest was added, and also feu duty (ground rent – in Scotland the land on which a house was built usually belonged to a 'superior') and the equivalent of council tax (2½% annually). Adam's 'Heirs and Assigns' were bound to repay the loan if it was still outstanding on his death.

Adam did not pay off the debt but in 1822 he made a settlement, in which he gave the house to his children equally[259]. This was the only way round the law by which the oldest son inherited all his father's property. Adam's wife Janet had the right to live there rent-free for life. He also obliged his other children to pay Adam junior twenty pounds a year between them, provided that he did not inherit any part of his estate excluding the property. He also required Robert senior, William, Agnes and Adam to pay his daughter Janet £25 over and above her share of the estate 'for the attention she has paid to me and my wife,' and appointed Robert to be Adam junior's tutor and custodian. Adam senior died some time before July 1823 because Robert went to court at that time to 'seise' the property on behalf of his sisters and brothers[260].

Adam lived long enough to see seven of his grandchildren: Daniel, Adam and Agnes McNeil and Janet and Helen McAlister (Agnes and Janet's children, respectively) and Robert senior's sons Robert and Alexander. Adam junior did not marry and nothing is known of William after he went to Demerara.

In 1824 Robert senior paid the full amount owed to Mrs Semple, who then renounced her ownership of the building 'for all time coming'[261]. It is clear from his will that it was all Robert senior's money and his brothers and sisters did not contribute.

By buying a house he could not pay for but binding his heirs to do so, Adam had ensured a roof over the heads of his widow, widowed daughter Janet and her children and his disabled son. He must have known that only Robert senior could repay the loan, but he still gave most of the house to his other children. Adam senior also owed his son Robert over £340 on current account at the time of his death, 'of which it is thought not more than £1 can be recovered.' This could be from loans Robert made to his father or from the long-term supply of provisions from the shop and suggests that Adam had not worked for quite a long time. An accident, failing eyesight or a disease like arthritis would make a physically demanding occupation impossible.

Robert senior had effectively paid for two houses but owned only a fifth of one. Even if Adam had set him up in the grocery business many years before, this treatment of his eldest son seems extraordinarily unfair. After Robert senior's death, the grocery had to support eight or perhaps nine people (his widow Jeannie and their three children, sister Janet and her two, brother Adam and his mother Janet, if she was still alive), though some of them could help in the shop.

14. Overstamped Spanish coin

There had been a shortage of silver coins in Scotland since the middle of the Eighteenth Century and after the Napoleonic wars the situation got worse. There were plenty of gold coins but change could not be given without silver and it was a considerable advantage to a trader to acquire some. Robert senior was one of only two men in Port Glasgow permitted to counterstamp Spanish silver coins which then became legal tender[262]. Unfortunately, no record of the town council's decision to allow him to do so exists. Such coins are so rare today that they have even been faked. The 'Robt Crighton Port Glasgow' stamp looks identical to that on the genuine coin, but the counterfeits have two additional, smaller stamps[263].

The Museum of Antiquities in Edinburgh bought one of the genuine coins in 1969/70, just before it was taken over by the

National Museum of Scotland. The latter no longer has a numismatic expert and the coin cannot now be found. It was minted in 1803 and overstamped about 1810. There is some disagreement about the value of 4/6 stamped onto the face – some say that is four shillings for the silver and six pence for Robert, others claim it is the value of the silver alone. Six pence Scots then would be about £2 now. The British Museum has a single example of the coin.

After Robert senior's death in 1828, Jeannie made an inventory of all his possessions and the money owed to him. Many of the shop's customers had a book or monthly account[264], which was how business was conducted in those days as well as being useful in a time of coin shortage. Two shipmasters owed a lot of money and others lesser amounts, suggesting Robert victualled ships:

Dugald McColl, Shipmaster Port Glasgow £101/2/6d
J. William Spence, Shipmaster there £84/13/2½d
John Burnett, Shipmaster there £16/5/4d

Jeannie, aged just thirty, was left a widow with three small children. The grocery represented security and Jeannie ran it as sole partner until her death. In addition she gradually bought property, becoming quite wealthy. In 1830 she paid part of a third party's loan secured on a house in Devol's Glen, and the rest in 1835 when the property became hers[265]. Paying off debts secured on property was a way of acquiring a house cheaply, in this case involving a wait of five years to complete the deal. She sold this house to James Gardner, sailcloth manufacturer, in 1843[266].

Jeannie's father Peter McKeich borrowed money in 1806, using his house in Kilmalcolm as surety[267]. In 1837 Jeannie repaid this debt (£125) with interest, regaining ownership of the house which she 'sold' to her daughter Margaret Lang Crighton for one hundred pounds in 1846[268]. Margaret was not married at the time and is unlikely to have had a hundred pounds. Her mother was making sure she always had a home (or an income from it), her brothers being at sea.

Peter McKeich borrowed money several other times with various properties as security, including his slate house in Port Glasgow (bought 1796) and another in Devol's Glen (not the one Jeannie redeemed) in 1803. When Peter died in 1816, this property reverted to the man who had made him the loan[269].

In 1840 Jeanie acquired most of a 999 year lease (called a tack) on a small cottage in Port Glasgow at a ground rent of three pence per year. The property turned out to be directly in the path of the Glasgow, Paisley and Greenock Railway Company's new line and in 1841 Jeannie was paid £65 for her right and interest in the tack, in order for the cottage to be demolished[270]. She was certainly a canny businesswoman.

Jeannie and her daughter Margaret moved to nearby 'Kilburn House, out Carnegie Way' (from Robert's obituary in the *Greenock Telegraph*) before the census of 1841. Carnegie was a large park on the edge of the Clyde, away from the overcrowded, dirty streets of Port Glasgow with its many public houses and rowdy sailors. The notice of Jeannie's death in the *Glasgow Herald* of January 23rd 1847 ends 'much respected'.

Appendix 1
Awards and Other Tributes

Very soon after details of the rescue were published, funds were set up all over America to collect contributions for rewarding the rescuers, who received medals, silverware and (in the case of the captains) large sums of money.

New York

As early as January 16th, the merchants of New York set up a committee to consider what form the testimonials should take and to start a fund. This eventually reached $17,000 which was distributed as follows[271] (reported January 24th, accounts vary slightly):

Captains Creighton, Low and Stouffer $2,500 each
First mates $250
Second mates $200
Petty officers $100
All other crew of the three ships $50
Each of these men was also to receive a medal.

It was felt that ready-made plate was not good enough for the occasion and instead the silverware should be commissioned, with special reference to appropriate design. This would, naturally, take time. It was finished by the end of December and displayed in the New York Exchange on March 1st 1855.

The three captains each received a gold medal, silver pitcher and tea service. The pitchers were ten inches tall and ornamented with nautical designs and scenes, one representing the wreck which is also on the medals. The gold medals were beautifully made, edged

15. Gold medal from the merchants of New York

with a rope design; Robert's is still in the family. On one side there is a picture of the rescue scene – a distressed person in the sea, a barrel and other flotsam are in the near foreground, with the *San Francisco* behind, though still with both paddle wheel housings. The two rescue ships are engraved beyond; the *Three Bells* is probably the one to the left as it only has a main sail. The turbulent sea is lit by and reflects the sun's fearsome rays quite magnificently. The medal presented to Robert is engraved:

> *Presented... by the MERCHANTS & CITIZENS of NEW YORK as a testimonial of their high sense of his perseverance and devotion in rescuing part of the passengers and crew of the U.S.Steamship San Francisco wrecked in the gale of 24th December 1853.*

The merchants of New York also made the following awards:

To the first mate of the *Three Bells*, Captain Pendleton and John
Marshall (1st engineer on the *San Francisco*) – gold medals
Crews of the three ships – silver medals
Captain Watkins – gold medal and a magnificent silver salver,
two pitchers and four goblets
Lieutenant Francis Murray of the Navy – a silver service
First officers of the Service – a gold medal
The total cost of all these awards was estimated to be about $7000

The Freedom of New York

Robert was presented with a snuff box and the Freedom of the
City on January 26th, 1854. The gold box is about eight-and-a-half
by six centimetres and three deep, richly chased and engraved:

*Presented to Captain Robert Crighton by the Common Council
of the City of New York, with the Freedom of the city for his
noble conduct in rescuing the lives of the passengers and crew
of the steamship San Francisco, which was shipwrecked in the
Gulf Stream, whilst bound from New York to San Francisco,
January 1854.*

New York Corn Exchange

It was reported in the *Baltimore Sun* that $4,106 had been
collected and distributed thus:

Captain Creighton $1,600
Captains Low and Stouffer (and one unreadable, probably
Pendleton) $800
The balance of $106 to be applied to the purchase of a gold
chronometer for each captain.

Baltimore

A committee passed resolutions tendering thanks to Captain Watkins, Major Wyse, Lieutenant Winder and others, requesting Congress to grant assistance to the widows and families of those who had perished and to set up a fund for testimonials to Captains Creighton, Lowe and Stouffer. By January 26th, this had reached $2000.

Boston

The committee of the Boston Marine Society passed a series of resolutions, including their approbation of the conduct of Captain Watkins and his crew in their efforts to save their ship, to keep up the spirits of the passengers and by their energy, courage and skill averted the sacrifice of hundreds of lives. It also resolved that the captains of the *Three Bells*, *Kilby* and *Antarctic*, and their crews were entitled to the grateful thanks of all American citizens, saying that 'in the palmy days of Greece and Rome they would not only have been richly rewarded but commemorated in bronze or marble at the public expense', and called for prompt and magnificent action of Congress.

The Committee of the Society sent a copy of these resolutions to the captains and also to Congress. They opened a fund for the captains, officers and crews of the three ships, adding that if any person wanted their contribution to go to the captains alone, this would be honoured. $6000 had been subscribed by 21st of January.

A meeting of Boston merchants was held on Jan 18th, with Mr Mellus present, to return thanks to the three captains, to ask Congress to deal quickly with the rescuers and with the needs of the sufferers and to receive funds. On 28th January the *Boston Daily Atlas* reported that $9,050 had been collected and distributed:

Captains Creighton, Lowe and Stouffer $1000 each
Officers of their three ships, according to rank $2,400 in total
Crews of the three ships $2,600 in total

Captain Watkins, his officers and crew, his engineer, Captain Pendleton and Lieutenant Murray $1050 to be divided between them.

Robert also received a magnificent silver tray.

The Marine Society of Boston and the Massachusetts Humane Society both presented medals to the three captains and others, including John Marshall.

The medal from the Massachusetts Humane Society has a rather odd illustration of a house called 'Succour' in the middle of the sea. In the background is a sailing ship which looks perilously near sinking, with hills beyond. In the foreground is a boat containing four people being propelled by a pole and pulled with a rope held by three men standing on a very small plank. Another man swims behind. The words 'Humane Society of Massachusetts Instituted 1785' appear round the edge.

On the reverse the inscription reads:

HONOR THE REWARD OF MERIT
To Capt. Robt. Crighton of the British Ship Three Bells
For his noble efforts in rescuing the passengers and crew of the
steamer San Francisco
Disabled at sea Dec 24th 1855
COURAGE AND PERSEVERANCE

Philadelphia

$10,000 was collected and distributed as follows:

Captain Crighton $2000
Captains Low and Stouffer $1000 each
Captain Pendleton $250
Captain Matthews of the *City of New York* $500 and a service
of plate

Lieutenant Murray $500
The balance to be divided between the officers and crews of
the three rescuing ships.

Gold medals were also awarded to the three captains, struck in
late 1854 according to Stacks (a major American coin and medal
dealer). Bronze replicas were made from 1861. One side has the
arms of the city, which includes a sailing ship. The inscription on
the reverse reads:

*Testimonial to Captains Crighton, Low and Stouffer of the ships
Three Bells, Kilby and Antarctic from the Corporation of the
City of Philadelphia for their gallantry in rescuing the passengers
from the wreck of the steamer San Francisco January 1854. The
San Francisco went down with the loss of 164 lives*

Robert also received another gold chronometer[272].

San Francisco

Resolutions were made by a Mr Brower that a committee be set
up to prepare testimonials to the Captains of the *Three Bells, Kilby,
Lucy Thompson* and the *Antarctic*, 'Whereas those who, regardless
of their own safety in their endeavours to save their fellow human
beings, deserve the praise of every lover of humanity throughout the
world [are] worthy of all praise, appearing as they did like ministering
angels'. These were to be sent to New York for presentation. This
was agreed but further details were not recorded.

Nationally

It was intended that the captains should receive silver trumpets from
the State Legislature. These would be speaking trumpets, used to magnify
the voice when giving orders or for communication between ships.

On February 7th 1854, Congress passed a Bill giving 'a sum not exceeding one hundred thousand dollars... to enable the President to award the officers and crews of those vessels that aided in the rescue', but the President (Franklin Pierce, reckoned by historians to be one of the least effective in the history of the United States) would not sign it. The trumpets were included in this Bill, so were probably never made.

Twelve years later, on July 26, 1866 the following resolutions were finally approved:

1. That the President of the United States be requested to procure three valuable gold medals with suitable devices, one to be presented to Captain Creighton of the ship *Three Bells*, of Glasgow; one to Captain Low, of the bark *Kilby*, of Boston; and one to Captain Stouffer, of the ship *Antarctic* etc.

2. The sum of seven thousand five hundred dollars is hereby appropriated to the above named captains respectively, as a reward of their humanity and heroism in the rescue of the survivors of the said wreck (and provision made for this sum to be given to the families if the captains had died).

3. To each mate the sum of five hundred dollars, and to each man and boy the sum of one hundred dollars (and to go to the families if the crew member had died)[273].

The Congressional Medal is America's most distinguished civilian award; only a few have been awarded to non-Americans. Those given to the three captains were called Congressional Lifesaving medals and were made of '320 pennyweight of pure gold' (about 500 grams), about two thousand dollars in value. Robert's was contained in a box made of bird's-eye maple with gold hinges, finished with black walnut and lined with blue velvet and satin. The medals were struck by the United States Mint from an engraving by Anthony C. Pacquet.

On the obverse there is a border of thirty-nine stars and the date. The central engraving is of a man and woman on a (very small) raft at sea, 'watching help coming' – a ship sailing towards them. The date on this side is July 26th 1866. The reverse shows an allegorical figure of America seated beside an eagle with the Capitol in the background, crowning a kneeling sailor with a laurel wreath. The medals were engraved:

> By joint resolution of Congress, to the rescuers of the passengers, officers and men of the steamship San Francisco, wrecked December 1853.

Robert's had the additional words:

> Testimonial of national gratitude for his gallant conduct. Capt Robert Creighton, ship Three Bells

There does not seem any doubt that Robert would have received the $7,500, directly by bill of exchange. Whether or not Robert received the money collected for him in 1854 is another matter.

The total sum raised to reward those involved in the rescue was $84,470 (excluding the medals and gold and silver items) to be distributed quite widely, not only to the three Captains. One paper reported that 'Much of the money which has been contributed for himself (Robert) and his crew by distant citizens of the Union, he will not see until sometime after he has arrived home'. Or, perhaps, ever.

In 1868 Robert commanded the *Venezuelan* which regularly called in at Aspinwall (Colon, Panama). The Panama correspondent of the *New York Herald* wrote a weekly column with details of ship's arrivals and departures and anything else he thought newsworthy. In June 1868 this was a meeting with Robert when they talked about the *San Francisco* tragedy[274]:

The old sea dog still sheds a tear over the loss of those whom he
was unable to save from that fearful wreck, and instead of seeking
praise for what he did only regrets his inability to do more.

The three captains had not received their Congressional Gold
Medals by May 1868[275] and the Panama reporter agitated for this to
be put right. Some months afterwards Robert was finally presented
with his (January 1869) and later showed the medal to his friend
who thought it 'a very beautiful specimen of workmanship'. This
meeting resulted in the appearance of a rather startling revelation
in the *New York Herald*, under the headline 'A Shameful Swindle'[276]:

The fact I am about to release has, I believe, never been made public,
and Captain Crighton himself, in the honesty and purity of his
heart, would never speak of it, The $25,000 was given to him and
remitted to Messers Finlay, Bell and Co. of Glasgow, on supposing
it would be safe with them, but conceive the Captain's astonishment
and disgust, on arriving home after a thirteen day's passage, and
applying for the amount, to be told that the money belonged to them
and not him as he was simply their employee... Captain Crighton
has never asked for the money since nor did he ever receive a dollar
of it. I hope it is not too late now, after a lapse of fifteen years to make
known in New York so contemptible an act... Captain Crighton I
am glad to say has outlived his loss and is just as happy, if not as
rich, as if he had the amount in his pocket. The transaction has not
dried up the milk of human kindness in his heart. He commands
a fine steamer now, and is still the whole-souled, generous and self-
sacrificing old sea-dog he was when he risked his life for eight days
to save the passengers and crew of a single ship.

$25,000 may be an exaggeration (the published amounts add
up to about $10,000) but it was still a very large sum of money.

Robert was given several cheques, in return for which either the Bell's agent in New York (if they had one) or a bank would issue bills of exchange[277], the usual method of currency conversion for international business at the time. Two, three or even more copies of these bills would be sent on different ships, the first to be cashed invalidating the rest. They were made payable to the Bells because the correspondent says the money 'was transmitted' to them[278]; Robert's trust was (apparently) badly misplaced.

An editorial in the *New York Herald* agreed with their Panama correspondent, 'It would be well... to try and recover from those who have wrongfully appropriated this fund, and have it restored to him for whom it was intended'[279], but nothing further was reported. It was probably just too long ago and in another country.

Over a hundred and thirty years later, the story was given some credence in a booklet celebrating two hundred years of trading by Wilson, Watson and McVinnie of Glasgow, now a catering company. Edward Watson, Sons and Co. Ltd bought John Bell & Sons in 1899 and as a result there are several pages about the company and the *Three Bells*:

> *Her rescue in 1853 of 200 US soldiers from a sinking steamer spread her fame across the Atlantic. The American Government gratefully acknowledged the rescue. They gave banquets in the skipper's honour and presented Captain Crichton with a £1000 reward. The Bell brothers, however, felt this money was rightfully theirs and took it from the Captain on the ship's return to port!*[280]

The booklet is not referenced, but the author remembers finding the information[281]. John Bell retired in 1885, having 'remained a devout church-goer all his life, not allowing the rise in his fortunes to change his thrifty and God-fearing ways'[282].

If this story is true, why did Robert not sue the Bells? He may not have been able to afford a lawyer (in 1854 he was still in debt to

James Lade) and losing such an action would have been disastrous, not only financially. This was mid – Nineteenth Century Scotland; ship owners were powerful people with friends in high places. If he lost he might never be given the command of another ship.

Although Robert did not sail the *Three Bells* again, he commanded the *John Bell* in 1859/60 which was half-owned by John Bell. It is difficult to believe that he would continue to work for someone who had denied him a fortune. Also, Robert's son born in 1863 was registered as William but always referred to as William Bell Crighton, which is odd if the Bells kept the money. Perhaps the verdict is that useful Scottish one, 'not (quite) proven'.

Robert said many times that he had only done his duty 'for humanity's sake' and expected nothing more than thanks from those he rescued. Both he and Edwin Low not only refused financial incentives at the time of the rescue, they were offended at the very suggestion that personal reward might make a difference to their actions. We can only applaud their sentiments, while at the same time thinking that if the story about the Bells is true they got away with a very mean-spirited act.

It was reported in the press that the shipping master at Glasgow had given £72.16.6d to the widows of Alex McBeath and another seaman whose exertions on the *Three Bells* cost them their lives. The money was said to have come from the people of New York, Philadelphia and Baltimore with the remainder from Captain Crighton and the crew of the *Three Bells*.

Where are all the medals, framed testimonials, letters and other non-financial awards now? Most of the items Robert had been given before he left New York in February 1854 were washed out of his cabin on the return journey back to Glasgow. These almost certainly included all the letters he had received, the written testimonials and the Freedom of New York. The silver pitcher and gold medal from the New York merchants were not presented until after March 1855, when they were exhibited in the Exchange. The former is probably now owned by the descendants of Robert's brother, Alexander, though the inscription has been removed[283]. The silver tray from the merchants of Boston, the snuff box and the beautiful gold medal from the merchants and citizens of New York passed to Robert's grandson William and are still owned by his family.

Robert's medal from the Humane Society of Massachusetts was sold by Stacks in 2004. It is not known where the chronometers he was given are today.

The whereabouts of the three Congressional Medals is also unknown (the one illustrated in *Shipwreck!* does not seem to be engraved with a name and is likely to be a replica). The official references to Robert's Congressional Medal spell his name Creighton. In the early reports of the tragedy it was spelled Crighton; it was only later that the 'e' crept in. Indeed, there is a published letter saying that a man destined to be a national hero should have his name correctly spelled; 'it is Creighton not Leighton'!

Other tributes

Poetry, songs and music were written about the rescue.

Poetry

The stanza from *'Song of Myself'* by Walt Whitman, published in *'Leaves of Grass'* in 1855.
The Three Bells by John Greenleaf Whittier.
For words, see Appendix 4. Whittier was a Quaker and an anti-slavery campaigner. He also wrote 'Dear Lord and Father of Mankind' and 'Immortal Love forever full'.

Music[284]

1. *The Three Bells Polka*, by T.J.Cook. The polka was a popular dance of the time and this tune is apparently quite difficult to play. There is a portrait of Robert at the top and a picture of the *Three Bells* with only two reefed sails racing towards the steamer. The dedication is

> *The gallant conduct of Captain Creighton of the ship Three Bells, in risking his own life to save those of his fellow-beings on board of the ill-fated San Francisco has won for him the admiration of the world and made him the object of innumerable honours and eulogies.*

2. *Four Bells Polka* (for piano) written by Miss Elizabeth Nelson and composed as a 'companion to the popular Three Bells Polka dedicated to Captn Creighton of the ship Three Bells.'
3. *The Antarctic, The Kilby and the Gallant Three Bells*. Song by James Brown (words) and John Daniel (music), New York, 1854.
4. *The Three Bells Quickstep* (1854) by the author of 'Sorrowful Katy'. On the cover is a picture of a sailing ship with the words 'The Noble Crighton'. Inside the dedication is to Lieut. Francis Key Murray, U.S.N.
5. *The Three Bells*, a song for baritone. The words by Whittier (see Appendix 4) set to music by Albert J. Holden, 1882.
6. *Three Bells*. A song by H.de Marsan, 1860, including:
   Let every man bless that good ship
   Brave Crighton's ship, Three Bells
   The words are surrounded by a colourful frame called the Trapper, the relevance of which is not apparent.

7. *The Wreck of the San Francisco.* 1854. On the cover is written 'Homage to the Noble Commanders Capts Lowe, Stouffer and Creighton'. It is scored for solo piano, with 'dramatic and descriptive scenery'. Indeed, the section called 'the gale' (*allego agitato*) actually depicts waves.

8. Ira D. Sankey was inspired to write the hymn *I'll stand by until the morning'* after the story of the rescue was related to him by a survivor[285].

9. There is also a piano solo with variations called *Three Bells*, published 1857 composed by Charles Grove but there is no dedication and it may be unconnected.

10. *'Be Cheery Boys, be Cheery,'* song and piano accompaniment by Wm J.Wetmore, undated. The front has a portrait of Robert and the words 'To Capt. Creighton of Bark Three Bells'.

As an obituary in an Australian newspaper said, 'No British sailor has been so lionised in America either before or since.'[286]

Appendix 2

The Court of Inquiry

Ordered by the U.S. President, Franklin Pierce, the inquiry had also been requested by Colonel Gates himself in answer to a letter from Captain Gardiner to the General-in-Chief of the Third Regiment which 'reflected disgracefully' on Gates' reputation. This could not pass unchallenged; the Colonel wanted 'ample justice' to be done.

Sitting only a few weeks after the disaster, on February 6th 1854, the court was held at the New York headquarters of Major-General Winfield Scott, who had earlier thanked Robert so warmly for his kindness to the troops. The main focus of the inquiry was the role and conduct of the army personnel and in particular Colonel Gates, who had a full support team[287].

Major Participants

The Court
Major-General Winfield Scott, Commander-in-Chief
Brigadier General Henry Stanton, Quartermaster's Department
Colonel E.V. Sumner, 1st Dragoons
Major John F. Lee, Judge Advocate
Colonel Shields, appearing for Colonel Gates

Third Regiment of Artillery
Colonel W Gates
Surgeon R Satterlee
Assistant Surgeon H. R. Wirtz
Major F. O. Wyse
Captain H.B. Judd

First Lieutenant S.L. Fremont
First Lieutenant L. Loeser
First Lieutenant W.A.Winder
First Lieutenant C. S. Winder
Second Lieutenant J. Van Voast
Second Lieutenant J. G. Chandler
Sergeant T McIntyre

Officers of the San Francisco
Captain J. Watkins
Mr F Mellus, First Officer
Dr W.P. Buel

Others
W. H. Aspinwall, one of the owners of the *San Francisco*
Captain J.W.T. Gardiner, First Dragoons
Lieutenant F. K. Murray, U. S. Navy
Colonel T. R. Swords, Quartermaster General's department
Chief Engineer W. H. Shock, U. S. Navy

Those in Colonel Gates' regiment had a delicate path to tread when giving their evidence. Lying under oath would imperil their immortal souls but an officer's first loyalty was to his regiment and his fellow officers. The inquiry had some elements of score settling and at times descended into farce.

The Commissioning

It was considered very important to get the Third Regiment to California as quickly as possible, so the *San Francisco* had been commissioned under pressure. The fact that she had not satisfactorily completed any trial, even in calm waters, was glossed over. Unfortunately the naval engineer, Mr W. Shock, who had tested the engines as well as he could, was ill immediately afterwards and could not be further consulted for some time. He had drawn attention to the 'novel contrivance' which was 'irregular in motion' but he did not object to the principle nor did he discover any 'lack of strength in the parts'. Metal fatigue (which probably caused the piston rod to break) was not known at the time. Indeed, 1854 was the year that the engineer John Braithwaite first coined the word 'fatigue' for failures in materials.

The vessel's depth in the water had been a matter of some concern, but this was thought to affect only speed, not safety. Lieutenant Fremont, for example, had remarked to Mr Aspinwall, Captain Watkins and Colonel Swords that the ship seemed to have settled rather low down and that was before the eight hundred tons of coal were loaded.

Embarkation and accommodation of the troops

About seven hundred men, laundresses, camp followers and children were embarked in a very short time. It was generally agreed that the men (approximately three hundred) accommodated on deck had suffered greatly from the cold but there was no alternative until space later became available as the stores were gradually used up. Mr Mellus, the ship's First Officer, disagreed. He thought those on deck and the paddle wheel guards had not suffered at all, contradicting Captain Judd who heard the men stamp and clap their hands all night to keep from freezing.

Lieutenant S.L.Fremont

Lieutenant Fremont was quite supportive of Colonel Gates, saying that he had not shown 'want of energy' in getting the ship bailed after she had been damaged, neither had he heard Captain Watkins ask the Colonel for any help. He added that a younger officer might have exerted himself 'more personally' had he been 'less incumbered (sic) with a family', but he did not think the men had suffered as a result. Also, some recruits had been very slow to obey orders and shirked work.

However, Lieutenant Fremont could not avoid admitting that the Colonel had left for the *Kilby* on the first (later thought to be the second) passenger boat and had given no orders regarding the transfer. Asked if the command should have been passed to Major Wyse on the *San Francisco*, the Lieutenant did not reply directly, saying he thought it was up to the Major.

Before the voyage started it was Fremont who had taken Dr Satterlee's letter regarding measles to the Colonel, who said that he regarded the disease as trivial and his children had to go with their parents. The Colonel had thrown away the letter unanswered, ignored the advice and taken his sick children aboard.

Other officers of the Third Regiment

Dr Buel (the ship's surgeon) diagnosed the disease aboard as definitely 'malignant cholera' that began after the *Kilby* parted company from the *San Francisco*, six days after the start of the storm. About seventy people died from it, including the fifteen who had been carried on to the *Three Bells* in a 'dying condition'. He thought everything which could have been done for the sufferers was done, under Major Wyse's command.

A major concern was that both army surgeons had boarded the *Kilby*. The injured Dr Satterlee had gone over to the *Kilby* in one of the first boats and Dr Wirtz had been asked to take some medicines over to him and had Wyse's consent to go.

Lieutenant Murray of the U.S. Navy regarded the *San Francisco* to have been in a proper condition to sail and attributed the wreck solely to the breakdown of the engines, specifically to the failure of the piston rod of the air pump. Before the engines stopped, he felt confidant the ship could ride out the storm. In his view the ship's officers received prompt and efficient help with the pumping.

Captain Judd said he had maintained comparatively good discipline without any orders from the Colonel who had spoken to him only to enquire about the fresh water pump. Once on the *Kilby*, he had taken it upon himself to ensure that the officer of the day had charge of the fresh water distribution since he did not regard the ship's steward as reliable. Judd was reluctant to comment about the distribution of food on the *Kilby*. He eventually said better arrangements could have been made for cooking the corn.

Quartered in the lower cabin with Colonel Gates on the *San Francisco*, Lieutenant Van Voast did not hear him give any instructions regarding aid for the ship's captain. The only orders he had received were from Major Wyse until Lieutenant Fremont told him to board the *Kilby* with ten men and to start jettisoning her cargo. Much later, when the officers and their families were being taken off the *Lucy Thompson*, Van Voast realised that no-one had been detailed to look after the troops left on board who were going straight to their barracks on Bledloe's Island. As Colonel Gates was leaving the ship, Van Voast asked for orders and was eventually told to stay with these men. The vacillation shown by Gates over this simple decision is a good example of the behaviour of someone deeply affected by grief.

Captain J. W. T. Gardiner

Captain Gardiner could and did speak more freely than the officers of the Third Regiment. His viewed the original embarkation as rushed and not in 'good military order'. Stunned by a blow to the head during the worst part of the storm, he was near Colonel Gates from 24th to 28th of December. During this time the Colonel's only orders were to bring him food and drink and he did nothing himself. The other officers worked on their own initiative. There should have been a system for issuing food and drink as well as for bailing the *San Francisco*. When the transfer to the *Kilby* started, Colonel Gates had said he would be the last to leave, though he was actually among the first. In fairness to Colonel Gates, Gardiner agreed that it could not have been foreseen that the ships would part company, but he thought the Colonel should have ensured that more food and water was transferred to the rescue ship by means of the hawser.

On the *Kilby* the only orders Gardiner received from Gates were requests for food and water. When he remonstrated with the Colonel for demanding more than his fair share of water, Gardiner was, somewhat shockingly, told '[I do] not care a damn for the men, I would rather twenty of them should die, than that my child should suffer'. In addition, although all could have corn from the hold, roasted or boiled in sea water, cooking arrangements had been chaotic and he thought the men had suffered as a result.

Major F. O. Wyse

Major Wyse was very critical of his commanding officer. Asked what neglect of duty he imputed to Gates, he replied that the Colonel had failed to make any details for bailing or lightening of the ship and taken no interest in the safety and comfort of his men. 'I would further state that had he been a citizen passenger, he could not have taken less interest in that command than he appeared to do.' He did not order water and provisions to be taken to the *Kilby*, nor get the surgeons to prioritise the sick and invalids to go first. He should have retained Captain Judd, Dr Wirtz and Lieutenants Fremont and Loeser on the *San Francisco*. He did not inform the next most senior officer (himself) that he was about to leave the wreck and gave him no orders.

Wyse had been left on the *San Francisco* with three lieutenants, 325 men and many of the camp women and their children. The only message he received from Gates on the *Kilby* was to send over some preserves for his children. The court ordered this to be struck from the record immediately but could not order the reporters not to publish it. There was laughter in court when it was revealed that the box sent over in response to this request had actually contained matches.

'Had the Colonel ever gone out of his cabin to see to the men and cheer them up?'

'Not one single time.'

'Could he have done so?'

'Yes'.

Wyse also seemed to doubt that Lieutenant W. A. Winder's seasickness (from the time he left New York until he returned) was genuine – perhaps the two men did not like each other – but Dr Satterlee later confirmed that Winder had received treatment for the illness.

On the sixth day of the Inquiry, Colonel Gates said that the presence on the *Kilby* of Lieutenants Fremont, Loeser, Van Voast, Captain Judd and Dr Wirtz was by his authority and he had not relinquished command to Major Wyse because he expected everyone would be transferred to the *Kilby*.

Mr Edward Mellus, First Officer of the San Francisco

Mr Mellus thought it doubtful the ship would have survived the storm even if the engines had continued to work. He described the broken air piston rod as four inches long and three wide. He said the ship's last trial was satisfactory (this was not actually true) and she was loaded more heavily than intended, but would have survived an ordinary gale.

Further examination of witnesses

Lieutenant Van Voast was recalled to answer extra questions and said he had taken charge of the drying of mattresses and blankets on the only fine day they had, and had discussed extending the life-ropes positioned round the deck. Major Wyse had spent less than a minute in the engine room and had twice given him orders. He did not hear Colonel Gates give any orders and the only work he saw him do was helping with the blankets.

Dr Wirtz was also recalled and said that Major Wyse had stayed in the cabin with the ladies most of the time and he had seen Lieutenants Van Voast, W.A.Winder and Chandler help lighten the ship.

Lieutenant W.A. Winder had seen the Colonel go forward for water on several occasions, which was dangerous. He had received orders twice from Major Wyse and had heard the Colonel give one order regarding the bailing.

Evidence for Colonel Gates

Two sergeants said the Colonel had assisted with nailing planks and oilcloth over a damaged companionway, to prevent water getting in. They had also seen him go for fresh water even when advised it was unsafe to do so and one had seen him use an axe to break up some debris. While on the *Kilby,* another sergeant had been detailed by the Colonel to jettison cotton.

The Band leader Joseph Horn said he had seen Colonel Gates go forward several times, heard him give orders to Lieutenant Fremont regarding bailing, request hourly reports on the state of the ship, order men to work who were staying with their families and ask about fresh water.

On the 'Kilby'

Sergeant McIntyre said he had given out the water ration every day on the *Kilby,* supervised by the officer of the day. All got the same and he did not hear Colonel Gates request additional supplies.

Captain Gardiner was asked if he had reported himself to the Colonel for orders while on the *Kilby* and replied, 'once only.' When asked why, he said, 'because Colonel Gates did not appear to take the slightest interest in his command. I did not report myself to anyone for orders, I made arrangements as I saw fit for the comfort of the men and the safety of the vessel'.

Lieutenant Fremont was then asked what Captain Gardiner had actually done regarding the security of the vessel and replied, 'nothing as far as I know' nor did he hear Gardiner give any orders regarding the comfort of the troops. Colonel Gates exercised no command after the wreck except when appealed to by the ladies and once regarding the bailing. Fremont thought the considerable confusion and danger on board the *San Francisco* had called for orders from the commanding officer.

Asked if he had ever reported to Colonel Gates for orders when officer of the day, Van Voast replied he had not because, 'there was no use in it. Colonel Gates, as I thought, took no interest in his command.'

Colonel Gates accuses Captain Gardiner.

Matters then took a different turn. In an attempt to discredit Captain Gardiner, Gates wrote to the court charging him with disgraceful conduct. Some ship's biscuits had been found in the *Kilby's* hold near where Gardiner had slept and he was accused of taking and secreting these without the consent of his commanding officer. A sergeant and five men were named as witnesses.

Captain Judd, who had slept near Gardiner, could explain the presence of the biscuits and did not bother to conceal his contempt at having to do so. Unable to eat for a few days after the rescue, he and his wife had saved about six biscuits in an unlocked box which was later taken into the hold and these were probably the ones that had been found. Judd added, 'with a heart overflowing with gratitude to Almighty God for our preservation... I never dreamed of being requested to explain the most trifling incident of our perilous trials to remove from a fellow-sufferer such an imputation'.

A further letter from Gates was read out, saying he had questioned Frederick Lincoln, one of the named witnesses, who had substantiated the charges but could not now be found. He attributed this to Captain Gardiner having bribed Lincoln to stay away.

Unfortunately for the Colonel, Lincoln was in court and gave evidence in spite of several attempts by Gates to prevent him from doing so. General Scott was clearly getting somewhat exasperated: 'If you brought him you cannot impeach him merely because his testimony is not what you expect'.

Which it was not. Under oath, Lincoln said Captain Gardiner had not given him any money and had in fact encouraged him to appear. This was backed up by a neutral witness who had seen and heard the brief conversation between the two men. The court was not interested in Lincoln's original evidence about the biscuits. Colonel Shields, head of the Colonel's defence team, then left.

Other witnesses said they knew some biscuits had been found in the hold, but not how they got there. Captain Gardiner had moved his sleeping place several times. Two men that Gates wished to question were not present: Sergeant McIntyre, to prove the bribery, and a Mr Felt who had found the biscuits. When McIntyre did eventually appear, he knew nothing of money being offered to Lincoln and the court decided that Felt could add nothing of significance.

There were a few further witnesses who had nothing material to add and Gates had to concede his allegations against Captain Gardiner were unproven. In making them he had further damaged his reputation.

The Colonel's defence statement

This was read to the court in Gates's absence. He seemed outraged that, instead of the sympathy he had expected, he was facing grave accusations in the press and by his fellow officers. His defence, naturally, made the most of the (slight) evidence in his favour and simply ignored the rest. Where this was not possible he refuted the criticism or offered an explanation of his actions. For example, he denied ever making the remark about not caring for his men. It had rained on the day he was supposed to have made it, so water had not been rationed. The alleged remark was 'in utter variance with my whole previous career both public and private'. He attributed Captain Gardiner's misinterpretation of his words to a 'morbid sensation produced by sickness and starvation', though Gardiner was not ill or starving at the time.

The Verdict

The court delivered its verdict in June. They found that the officers who had selected the *San Francisco* had every reason to believe she was a 'good and sufficient' transport for the troops and that the embarkation was orderly and reasonable. The failure of the expedition was caused by a storm of extraordinary violence and the breaking of a piston rod. There was no insubordination but they found 'with pain' that there was blameable disorganisation by Colonel Gates 'notwithstanding the loss of an interesting son' (an odd adjective). Colonel Gates had been alive only to 'his own immediate wants and those of his family' and had taken the first chance to escape, leaving his junior officers 'supplying his deficiencies'. The court specially recommended Lieutenants Van Voast, C. S. Winder, Chandler and Major Wyse. Junior officers had also to take command on the *Kilby* and Captain Gardiner and Van Voast were commended.

Two of Colonel Gates' actions were found to be particularly 'selfish and censurable'. These were taking his sick children on board against medical advice, threatening the lives of others, and his declaration (with an oath) that he did not care if his men died of dehydration. The Colonel's charges against Captain Gardiner were entirely groundless and seemed to have originated in 'a spirit of gross malignancy'[288]

Courts of Inquiry did not pass sentence but the Colonel never again commanded the regiment. He was 'awaiting orders' until 1861 and then on gardening leave until his retirement in 1863. Two years after retiring, he was promoted to brigadier, by which time he was over eighty years old[289].

Another (personal) view

The army's role in the tragedy was completely whitewashed in the inquiry's findings. The *San Francisco* was far from being a 'good and sufficient' transport, even before being well overloaded. Her hull was very strong or she would have broken up during the days of relentless pounding but the engines had never worked properly. The officers who commissioned her were extraordinarily negligent and the owners also bear considerable responsibility because they knew that the *San Francisco* had not passed her sea trials but still tendered for the contract. How was it that Lucia Eaton, a young woman who had no experience of sea-going, was the only person known to have had grave doubts about the safety of the ship after witnessing her being towed into port?

Why was Captain Watkins satisfied with the condition of the ship's engines and unconcerned about the overloading? Why were there apparently no spare parts for the engines on board and why were there no questions about this during the inquiry? Why were no extra sails stowed in the hold for safety (although there were some on deck because a few soldiers slept on them)? Crews of sailing ships on long voyages frequently included a sailmaker and a carpenter and materials for repairs and replacements; naval ships might carry a blacksmith as well. The broken piston rod was made of cast iron sheathed in brass, which probably could not be replicated on board; all the more reason to carry spares.

Very little notice was taken of the fact that Colonel Gates had just lost his eldest son, Charles, in dreadful circumstances. He exhibited classic symptoms of grief yet was not shown any compassion. Of course, as the senior officer of the regiment, he should have directed, looked after and encouraged his men and should not have been so dismissive of the surgeon's concerns about the measles, but he was made a scapegoat for the major failings of his superiors.

The sequel

The regiment was still needed in California and in April Major Wyse was ordered to take four companies of the reorganised regiment and the band to their original destination aboard the *Falcon*. The army had learned nothing because there were questions about this ship's seaworthiness also and Wyse refused to go. He was proved right. The steamer's engines broke down soon after the *Falcon* left port and she only just managed to limp to safety before a storm broke. Lieutenant Loeser took over command of the regiment which eventually completed the journey on the *Illinois*. Lucia did not accompany her sister on this occasion and no more is known of her.

Wyse faced a court-martial and was, inevitably, found guilty of disobeying orders and sentenced to be dismissed the service. However, on the unanimous recommendation of the officers trying him, the President commuted this to six months' loss of rank, command and pay.

The story of the wreck could be made into a great film, perhaps from the point of view of Lieutenant Lucien Loeser. Having gone to California by sea in 1846, a journey that took six months, he was in California when gold was discovered in 1848. Selected to carry the historic despatches announcing this discovery to Washington, he made the journey in four months via Peru, Panama, Jamaica and New Orleans. He then served as a garrison officer in various barracks until the voyage on the *San Francisco* and commanded the regiment when it again set off for California. He was still working as Chief of the Record Division of the New York Custom House when he died in 1897 aged seventy-nine[290].

Appendix 3

Robert's Financial Affairs

One aspect of Robert's life about which there are intriguing hints but few answers is his relationship with money.

Robert was twenty-five years old when his mother Jeannie died in January 1847. Written just a week before, her will shows an advance to Robert of £350 though not when this advance was made. Robert had been fully employed and was unmarried so when and why did he need such a large sum of money, enough to buy a house? In the absence of hard evidence it is only possible to make an informed guess.

Although Robert was employed on the *Cingalese* in 1843, there was a slump in the shipping trade that year which was ended by the 'guano rush'. Suddenly idle vessels were sent to South America and West Africa to collect the 'white gold' and this was a great chance for Robert to secure his first command, especially if he was a part-owner of the ship. This is one possible use for the advance.

Jeannie had the money from the 1843 sale of one of her properties (if this was not enough, she also had the business) to give Robert his advance before he set off in April 1844 as master of the *Roseanna*. Captains needed some high quality instruments including a telescope, sextant and chronometer, and weapons such as pistols and swords to defend themselves against pirates. They also had a 'slop chest' from which they sold 'luxuries' to the crew, such as clothes, soap and tobacco. The cost of these, plus a little extra for the captain, was deducted from a man's pay at the end of a voyage but would have involved an outlay before a first command[291].

Another explanation of his need for the cash is that shipmasters could carry some cargo on their own account and Robert might have used part of the advance for this, especially when he went to the Far East.

In March 1847 Robert claimed his father's one-fifth of the King Street property, though not appearing in person because he was at sea[292]. Unlike his father Adam, Robert senior had not made a settlement so, by law, his entire share of the house passed to his eldest son on his death – although Jeannie had the right to stay there for her lifetime. On April 20th, Robert, Margaret and Alexander 'seised' – one-third each of their father's one-fifth. Robert need not have bothered being so fair – his brother and sister never sold their small fractions.

In 1849, Robert applied for and was granted the two one-fifth shares once belonging to his uncles, William and Adam[293], and thus owned seven-fifteenths of the building (three-fifteenths from each uncle and his own one-fifteenth). He apparently sold his fraction of the property in 1850[294] though no purchase price was mentioned in the document. A further sasine of 1863[295] makes it clear that this was not actually a sale but in security for 'certain cash advances made by James Lade to the said Robert Crighton and business accounts due by the said Robert Crighton to the said James Lade'. Lade was both a Procurator Fiscal of Greenock and a writer (solicitor) in Port Glasgow, with an office in the King Street property. After James died in 1859, Robert still owed him £53/8/8d, the balance of the rent/loan/account/interest equation. With further interest and expenses this had increased to £98/0/8d in 1863, which was paid by John Anderson to Lade's heirs, John thus acquiring Robert's share of the property. He later bought the shares settled on Adam's daughters and then owned thirteen-fifteenths of the whole i.e. everything except the small fractions belonging to Alexander and Margaret.

The 'business accounts' were probably left over from Jeannie's death. Robert and two of James Lade's apprentices made an inventory of all her possessions and sold the stock of the shop. All the customer's debts had to be collected, a time-consuming business which could not have been done by Robert because he was at sea. Even allowing payment for Lade's services as a writer Robert must have borrowed quite a lot in 1850, because the ten year's rent to 1860 was not sufficient to cover the accounts and loan with interest.

The loan was probably needed to square things financially with his family after his mother died. In her will Jeannie wrote that Robert was to account to Alexander and Margaret for their share of the grocery business, equal to his advance, without interest. Her estate was valued at £532. Even if all the creditors paid what they owed, the shortfall was still £168 and at the time Robert was earning only about £10 a month[296] (although he may have supplemented his income by carrying some cargo on his own account and from the 'slop chest'). The length of time between Jeannie's death and the loan/settlement may have been due to attempts to trace the debtors and get them to pay.

There is another, much less likely, reason for the loan. The date of the 1850 sasine is May 1st, which is after Robert returned home from his first voyage on the *Zarah*. Some of the cotton in her hold had been damaged by sea water and was auctioned for whatever it would raise. Captains were held liable for any damage to their cargoes unless due to piracy or an Act of God.

Any financial problems he had should have been over after a small fortune was collected for him in America after the rescue, but, if we believe the correspondent of the *New York Herald* and the author of *Wilson, Watson and McVinnie*, the Bells kept the money. It seems not a little ironic that Robert protested all along that he had done no more than his duty and had expected only the thanks of those he had rescued. If he did receive the money, why did he not settle his debt with James Lade or buy a house for his growing family, perhaps with an eye to his eventual retirement?

Robert was awarded $7,500 by Congress in 1866 and this money probably supported the family in the early 1870s, when he described himself as a master mariner but was not at sea.

Robert does not seem to have been very successful as a ship's agent, since one partnership was dissolved in 1864 and he gave up the agencies and returned to sea in 1867. The family lived in four different houses in Birkenhead, from St. George's View through Hawthorn Villas and New Chester Road to a small terraced house in Victoria Road, which constitutes definite downsizing.

For the last years of his life Robert had a steady income as Marine Superintendent of the Red Star Line and may have put some capital (along with his name) into the Béliard Crighton Company in Antwerp. He did not leave a will.

Appendix 4
The Three Bells

BENEATH *the low-hung night cloud*
That raked her splintering mast
The good ship settled slowly,
The cruel leak gained fast.

Over the awful ocean
Her signal guns pealed out.
Dear God! was that Thy answer
From the horror round about?

A voice came down the wild wind,
'Ho! ship ahoy!' its cry
'Our stout Three Bells of Glasgow
Shall lay till daylight by!'

Hour after hour crept slowly,
Yet on the heaving swells
Tossed up and down the ship-lights,
The lights of the Three Bells!

And ship to ship made signals,
Man answered back to man,
While oft, to cheer and hearten,
The Three Bells nearer ran;

And the captain from her taffrail
Sent down his hopeful cry
'Take heart! Hold on!' he shouted;
'The Three Bells shall lay by!'

All night across the waters
The tossing lights shone clear;
All night from reeling taffrail
The Three Bells sent her cheer.

And when the dreary watches
Of storm and darkness passed,
Just as the wreck lurched under,
All souls were saved at last.

Sail on, Three Bells, forever,
In grateful memory sail!
Ring on, Three Bells of rescue,
Above the wave and gale!

Type of the Love eternal,
Repeat the Master's cry,
As tossing through our darkness
The lights of God draw nigh!

John Greenleaf Whittier *1872*

Ironically, 1872 is the year the *Three Bells* was 'recommended to be sold' (presumably for scrap), having been ice-bound in the St Lawrence River, December 1871.

List of Robert's ships

*Name — Type — Tonnage — Home Port — Captain (if not
Robert) or ship's number*

Leguan — Full rigger — 349 — Glasgow — W.Spence
Helen — Hamilton — 203 — Liverpool — A.Nicol
Cingalese — Barque — 252 — Liverpool — Hutchinson
Roseanna — Barque — 397 — London then Greenock
Amelia* — Schooner — 240 — Glasgow
Zarah — Barque — 357 — Glasgow — 11543
Three Bells — Clipper — 648 — Glasgow — 11948
Tornado — Clipper — 1220/9 — Glasgow — 31789
John Bell — Clipper — 997 — Glasgow — 24658
Crusader — screw steamer — 725 — Liverpool — 44664
Venezuelan — screw steamer — 1347 — Liverpool — 29980

*Note: there are so many ships called *Amelia* that this data is only
a best guess.

Endnotes and References

Archives

CL   Caird Library, National Maritime Museum, Greenwich London

ML   Mariner's List www.mariners@rootsweb.com. Searchable at www.ancestry.co.uk

NA   National Archives, Kew, London

NAS   National Archives of Scotland, Edinburgh

1. The exact wording, spelling and punctuation of *Leaves of Grass* varies slightly, depending on the edition and the source.
2. Hood (2006) 355
3. As well as the 185 people he rescued, Robert attracted the attention of the *Antarctic* to the wreck, by which another 175 or 6 were saved (*Liverpool Mercury* January 24th 1854).
4. Anon (2009)
5. www.admiraltylawguide.com/documents/oleron.html
6. Bowie (undated) 1-2
7. Betty Hendry, Watt Library, Greenock. Personal communication.
8. This paragraph is a mixture of memories of small shops in rural Ireland in the early 1950s and research on the brewing and sugar trades.
9. E.g. NAS RS54/685/265
10. Anon (2009) 11
11. www.portglasgow4u.org had a great deal of information about Port Glasgow's history but has disappeared.

12. Macarthur (1932)
13. Anon (2009) 81
14. Johnston (2007) 124
15. Macarthur (1832)
16. Anon (2009) 81
17. e.g. Faed, Thomas (1849) *Boyhood*
18. That is, could handle sails and ropes, reef (roll up) the sails in bad weather and steer the ship. Sailors rated themselves but were soon discovered if they claimed to be able when they were not and their pay reduced.
19. Watts (2002) 85-87
20. From the Aubrey/Maturin books of Patrick O'Brian.
21. Crompton (2011) 36 for example.
22. Woodman, R (2009) 53
23. The list of Robert's early ships is held at CL and can also been seen on www.ancestry.co.uk.
24. Royal Commission, 1842: Report on Children in Mines.
25. After the abolition, field slaves became apprentices for a further six years, during which time they were paid only for the hours they worked in excess of forty-five a week.
26. All arrivals and departures of merchant quoted were listed in local and London newspapers. They can be found in the database *19th Century British Library Newspapers.*
27. *The Belfast News-Letter* September 19th 1860
28. *Liverpool Mercury* June 18th 1841
29. Gleig (1879)
30. The common spelling of the city at the time.
31. *Caledonian Mercury* July 12th 1842, *Morning Chronicle* July 18th 1842
32. *Caledonian Mercury* October 9th 1843
33. McCalman (1787)

34. Van der Burg, P.H. *Malaria in Batavia in the Eighteenth Century.* Tropical Medicine and International Health 2 892-902

35. Woodman (2009) 79 *et seq*

36. *Ibid* 34

37. *Ibid* 63

38. http://web.uct.ac.za/depts/stats/adu/ichaboe.htm

39. Snyders,H. and Swart,S (2013): *Discontented scoundrels who crowd the mercantile marine today – labour relations regimes of the Cape and Ichaboe guano trade.* Historia 58 51-75

40. *The Standard* September 17th 1844

41. *Bristol Mercury* September 21st 1844

42. *Ibid* July 6th 1844

43. *Morning Post* October 7th 1844

44. *Glasgow Herald* January 10th 1845

45. *Lloyd's Register of Ships* 1846 has 'srprs 45', which translates to 'some repairs 1845'.

46. Woodman (2009) Chapter 2, Lubbock(1933), www.victorianweb. org/history/empire/opiumwars/opiumwars1.html

47. Woodman (2009) 84

48. *Ibid* 107

49. http://www.coalfire.caf.dlr.de/media/download/results/ StudyWP2410a6.pdf

50. *Glasgow Herald* March 14th 1845

51. Scottish wills are available at www.scotlandspeople.gov.uk Also births, marriages and deaths from 1855 and old parish records before then.

52. *Lloyds London Weekly Newspaper* June 27th 1847

53. ML April 30th 2014

54. There was another ship with the name *Zarah* trading with the Far East at the time.

55. *The Standard* September 20th 1851

56. Watts (2002) 37

57. *Morning Chronicle* November 14[th]1851

58. Druett (1998)

59. www.howardscott.net/4/Shameen_A_Colonial_Heritage/Files/Journal.html

60. Druett (1998)

61. McGarry, (2006) 174

62. This could take four hours, Crompton (1866) 29

63. The primary source for information about the *San Francisco* tragedy is the *New York Daily Times,* especially the editions of January 14th and 16th 1854. The timing of events is that given on January 14th by an unnamed officer of the *San Francisco*. There is some confusion about this, probably because a ship's day ran from noon to noon. Other publications referred to: Stackpole (1977) Crighton (1985), Taylor-Leigh (2007) (Part 2 only) and Hood (2006) 180-207. Much further information is contained in the newspaper reports of the Inquiry into the loss of the *San Francisco* (Appendix 2).

64. Taylor-Leigh (2007) 153

65. When I sought permission to reproduce this advertisement, I was asked if I had placed it myself!

66. Crew Agreement and list of cargo kindly supplied by Jim Bell.

67. Lucia Eaton's manuscript is in the library of the Marine Historical Association (now called Mystic Seaport). The narrative is contained in Stackpole (1977) and Taylor-Leigh (2007).

68. *Baltimore Sun* January 17th 1854

69. This number varies according to the authority from 120 to 200. 140 is probably closest to the truth.

70. Taylor-Leigh (2007) 135

71. Anon (undated) 9

72. Thirty-two and some officers was reported.

73. Or, perhaps, just thrown overboard.

74. *New York Daily Times* January 28th 1854

75. The behaviour of the Colonel and other officers on the *San Francisco* was investigated in the inquiry, Appendix 2.

76. *Daily Cleveland Herald* January 26th 1854

77. Including by Florence Nightingale until her death in 1910.

78. Hempel (2006) 223

79. *Ibid* 45. Almost unbelievably, the 'treatments' included pouring boiling water over the abdomen and bleeding, purging and giving strong emetics to already dehydrated bodies.

80. Crighton (1985) 27

81. There is some variation in the order of events and wording of messages, according to who recorded them.

82. Hood (2007) 197

83. Anon (undated) 12

84. The First Officer of the *San Francisco*, Edward Mellus denied the scuttling but it would have been normal practice to do so.

85. *Boston Daily Atlas* 2nd and 3rd January 1854

86. *Liverpool Mercury* January 24th 1854

87. *Georgia Telegraph* January 10th 1854

88. Anon (undated)

89. Anon (undated) 12

90. *New Hampshire Statesman* January 28th 1854. Cholera was often misdiagnosed, which may account for the stewardess's opinion.

91. *Morning Chronicle* January 26th 1854

92. Hood (2007) 203

93. Stackpole (1977) 246

94. *Liverpool Mercury* January 27th 1854

95. Lucia Eaton's narrative (ref 53), supplemented with reports of the inquiry, held in February 1854 (Appendix 2) and published verbatim in the *New York Times*.

96. *New York Daily Times* January 16th 1854, 8

97. *New Hampshire Statesman* January 21st 1854

98. *The Ripley Bee* (Georgetown, Ohio) February 4th 1854

99. *The Times* (London) August 20th 1858 and August 13th 1859

100. *The Standard* February 9th 1857

101. *Morning Oregonian* February 3rd 1898

102. *New York Daily Times* January 16th 1854

103. *New York Daily Times* January 14th 1854

104. Most of the information about Robert's time in America was printed in the *New York Daily Times*.

105. Stackpole (1977) 59

106. The blood of cholera sufferers does eventually look black from concentration.

107. *Ohio Observer* February 1st 1854

108. This was probably to ensure the crew did not desert in New York.

109. *New Hampshire Statesman* January 21st 1854

110. Information supplied by the Grand Lodge of New York via Robert D.L.Cooper of the Grand Lodge of Scotland. Also Balestier, J.N. (1862 and 1878) *Historical Sketches of Holland Lodge,* New York: the Lodge.

111. *New York Daily Times,* January 16th 1854

112. *Vermont Chronicle* February 7th 1854

113. *New York Daily Times* January 23rd 1854

114. *Daily National Intelligencer* (Washington) January 27th 1854

115. *New York Daily Times* January 25th 1854

116. Margaret Parker identified herself being employed by the Taylors as a nurse. If she had been an adopted daughter (Taylor-Leigh [2007] 13) she would have shared the Taylor's suite and died with them.

117. *Weekly Herald* January 28th 1854

118. *New York Daily Times* January 27th 1854

119. www.twainquotes.com/Muscatine/18540217.html

120. E.g. *New York Daily Times* January 31st 1854

121. *North American and United States Gazette* (Philadelphia) February 3rd 1854

122. *Boston Investigator* February 18th 1854

123. *The Daily Register* (Raleigh NC) February 22nd 1854

124. *Boston Daily Atlas* February 16th 1854

125. *Ibid* February 8th 1854

126. *North American and United States Gazette* May 18th 1854

127. *The Daily Register* (Raleigh NC) February 22nd 1854

128. *Daily National Intelligencer* February 24th 1854

129. Cargo list supplied by Jim Bell.

130. *North American and United States Gazette* April 7th 1854

131. *Glasgow Herald* January 30th 1854

132. *Ibid* March 10th 1854

133. Angus Huck and Jim Bell, personal communications

134. Jim Bell, personal communication

135. Hollett (1986). There was another ship called the *Tornado*, operating from Liverpool to Sydney, Captain Mumford, at the same time as the *Tornado* captained by Robert. Hollett mixes up the two ships.

136. www.liverpoolmuseums.org.uk

137. *Glasgow Herald* March 9th 1855

138. NA BT98/4211

139. *The Argus* August 21st 1855

140. www.westonaprice.org/environmental-toxins/beatiful-black-poison

141. NA BT98/5482

142. The cargo list was compiled from sales advertisements, e.g. *The Argus* (Melbourne) September 15th 1856

143. *The Argus* September 15th 1856

144. *Ibid* September 19th 1856

145. *Ibid* October 28th and 31st and November 3rd 1856

146. Wilson, Benjamin G. (undated): *Diary of a Medical Parson from Hoy*. Extracts from the manuscript published in the *Ulster Link*, Australia, 1980, March/April, May/June, July/Aug.

147. www.iranicaonline.org/articles/anglo-persian-war-1856-57

148. The *Cheshire Observer* of July 4th reported that the 64th and 78th regiments had landed in Bombay the previous weekend and were immediately sent to Calcutta.

149. There is some confusion as to whether this man's Christian name was John or William. There is only one 'Steel' in the crew list, who signed on as William.

150. Wilson (undated) See note 133

151. NA BT98/6170

152. *Ibid*, log book

153. Transportation!

154. *The Argus* December 10th 1858

155. *Ibid* December 15th 1858

156. *The Polynesian* October 14th 1848

157. This is the value of the gold in pounds sterling (l as in lsd).

158. *Glasgow Herald* March 9th 1859

159. *Newcastle Courant* April 8th 1859

160. *Daily Southern Cross* October 11th 1859

161. *Morning Chronicle* August 18th 1860

162. Much of the information in this chapter is contained in a privately printed booklet: Jim Bell (2012) *The Ship John Bell*.

163. *Glasgow Herald* October 1st 1856

164. *Falmouth Gazette* July 17th 1857

165. This is available at www.ancestry.co.uk

166. All the crew log books and agreements for the *John Bell* are at NA BT98/6085.

Pay List, per month.
Neil M. McDougal 1st Engineer £18
John McGregor 2nd Engineer £9

Firemen £15
Seaman (aged 20) £3
Seaman (aged 16) £1/10/0
Boy (aged 15) 1/-
James Fleming 1ˢᵗ Steward £6
2ⁿᵈ " £3/10/0
Andrew Waller Baker £2/10/0
The firemen were all on equal pay.

167. *Glasgow Herald* July 7ᵗʰ 1859
168. *Ibid* August 18ᵗʰ 1859.The dates in the crew log book and the newspaper announcement differ slightly.
169. *Glasgow Herald* November 4ᵗʰ 1859
170. *New York Daily Tribune* December 6ᵗʰ 1859
171. *Glasgow Herald* February 7ᵗʰ 1860
172. Post Office Directory for Glasgow, 1860-1861
173. 1861 census. Govan;ED:14;page 13;line 6; Roll CSSCT 1861-114
174. www.liverpoolmuseums.org.uk/
175. www.liverpooldiscovers.co.uk
176. English birth and death certificates can be obtained from the local Register Office or (by post or in person) from the General Record Office.
177. NAS RS 54/1679/274
178. University of Georgetown, Washington. Manuscript Collection GTM.GAMMS194
179. Massett, S.C. (1863): *Drifting About.* New York: Carleton
180. I was born and brought up in Birkenhead, where my father worked for Cammell Laird, always called Lairds. WW11 bombing had left great gaps in streets where children played in the gutter wearing perhaps a torn vest and a pair of black gym-shoes. A few years ago I went back, searching for another

family whose sons had left Tetbury to brew beer in the boom town. Although the houses have been rebuilt and the children are better clothed, Birkenhead is not a place to which I ever want to return. Also www.wirralhistory.net, www.clbh.co.uk, www.birkenheadhistorysociety.org.uk

181. *Liverpool Mercury* March 30th 1866
182. Pelzer, John D. (1990): *Liverpool and the American Civil War*. History Today 40 (3). On-line at www.historytoday.com
183. *Jamaican Gleaner* February and July 18th 1866, September 12th and 23rd 1867
184. *Liverpool Mercury* July 2nd 1868
185. *Jamaican Gleaner* September 2nd 1868
186. *Liverpool Mercury* October 1st 1868
187. *Ibid* January 26th 1869
188. *Glasgow Herald* February 1st 1869 reprinted from the *Norfolk Virginian* January 14th. By the time the *Liverpool Mercury* of February 18th reported the story, Robert had rescued 650 people, the *Three Bells* had been making nine inches of water an hour and the medal weighed 'over 14 ounces'!
189. *Liverpool Mercury* March 9th 1869
190. *Ibid* August 10th 1869
191. *North American and United States Gazette* April 16th 1872
192. Finch (1988)
193. Pateman (1989) 31, quoting the *Greenock Advertiser* March 11th 1856
194. *North American and United States Gazette* August 2nd 1873
195. From an obituary in the *Morning Post*, December 1st 1882
196. ML
197. The police immigration records in Antwerp names all the Crighton family and gives their address.

198. The Statutory Registers of births, marriages and deaths in Scotland after 1ˢᵗ January 1855 are accessible through www. scotlandspeople.gov.uk

199. www.memento-mori.co.uk/43.pdf John's surname and date of death have been mistranscribed

200. A medal commemorating 50 years of Béliard Crighton, 1877-1927 was recently offered for sale. More research is needed about the early history of the company and the Crighton family's connection with it.

201. Mates and Master's Certificates are held at the CL (but a fortnight's notice is required to see them) and on-line at www. ancestry.co.uk

202. Rijksarchief te Antwerpen

202. Obituaries were published all over the world. In the *Morning Post* of December 1ˢᵗ 1882, the number he rescued had grown to seven hundred and the *Three Bells* had stood by for more than a week. A small sample of other obituaries: the *Dundee Courier* December 05, the Daily Evening Bulletin (San Francisco) December 27ᵗʰ 1882, the *Narracoorfe Herald* (South Australia) April 24ᵗʰ 1883 and finally the *Queenslander* May 12ᵗʰ 1883.

203. *Northern Argus* April 17ᵗʰ 1883

204. 1901 census RG13/481/164/6

205. *Port Glasgow Express and Observer* December 11ᵗʰ 1909

206. The red granite memorial can be found in the graveyard opposite the newer church in Monken Hadley.

207. *New York Daily Times* January 17ᵗʰ 1854

208. *Greenock Telegraph* December 2ⁿᵈ 1882

209. *Jamaican Gleaner* August 4ᵗʰ 1869

210. *The Shipbuilder* (1924) 31, 208 (obituary)

211. Information by kindness of the owner, Michel Van Hentenrijk.

212. NA WO339/31470

213. *Glasgow Herald* August 3ʳᵈ 1889

214. *Daily Pecayune* (New Orleans) February 4th 1890
215. From his death certificate.
216. From Antwerp police records.
217. *The Times* March 22nd 1957
218. Funeral address, personal communication James Deane.
219. *The Times* April 13th 1961
220. Information about Alfred's prizes at the Dollar Academy kindly supplied by their archivist Mrs Janet Carolan.
221. Antwerp police records.
222. From the application for his mate's certificate, held by CL and can be seen on www.ancestry.co.uk
223. The *Launceston Advertiser* (Tasmania) November 2nd 1843 and *The Australian* November 9th 1843
224. The Creighton family in America supplied information about Alexander's life on Grand Cayman.
225. Hirst (1910) IV 255
226. Death certificate kindly supplied by Carol Mascarenlas, www.gov.ky
227. www.caymantripper.com
228. Story from Alexander's descendants in America.
229. Harvey, D.G (1924): The Argyle Settlement in History and Story. Beloit, Wisconsin: Daily News Publishing Co., www.ralstongenealogy.com/argylscot.htm
230. www.enclycopedia.chicagohistory.org. There are different opinions about when Chicago became a city. I apologise if I have offended anyone by suggesting gambling.
231. Or if he did, he did not claim it as sea-going experience.
232. www.stuff.co.nz/sport/opinion/5914910/Gambling
233. Alexander may also have planned to use an inheritance from his mother, but neither the amount nor the timing was defined in 1839!

234. *Southern Patriot* (Charleston) November 12th 1839, *Spectator* (NY) March 3rd 1841, *Chicago American* reprinted in the *Commercial Advertiser* (NY) January 8th 1841

235. This information was collated from successive censuses and death certificates.

236. NAS RS 114/27/190

237. A letter written by Robert Alexander Crighton Thomson saying he was the last Crighton (in Britain?) implies that his brothers had died without heirs (letter dated 3rd February 1933, RACT to his cousin Alexander M. Crighton, junior on Grand Cayman).

238. All references to parish registers and wills in Scotland prior to 1855 were found at www.scotlandspeople.gov.uk

239. Hirst (1910) IV 254

240. NAS. Sasine Abridgements for Lanarkshire 1783, 382 and 414 and 1786, 856

241. Lanarkshire Family History Society (ND) Hamilton Parish Churchyard, Monumental Inscriptions

242. NAS PR 32.59

243. www.jamaicanfamilysearch.com This Robert Crighton had a son Robert, who was a carpenter (as James was on marriage).

244. NAS RS 54/1109/43

245. Weir (1829) 8

246. Betty Hendry, Watt Library, Greenock, personal communication

247. Although the most likely baptism of Adam Crighton is 1749, there is another possibility. No Crighton (or variant names) baptisms or marriages were recorded in Greenock at all for the 1760s, which seems very odd as there were several families of that name in the town before and after that decade. Perhaps there were two men called Adam Crighton, uncle and nephew, the sailmaker being born about 1765 to the man shown on the chart as Adam's bother, John. There is enough time, forty-

one years, for three generations – John born 1787, son of Adam born (say) 1865 son of John born 1845. The baptisms of both Johns are known. This fits with Adam (sailmaker) calling his eldest son John (after his father) but assumes another unrecorded baptism.

248. NAS CH2/1418

249. The description of life in Greenock is blended from Weir (1829) and Smith (1921).

250. Baird, Thomas (1840): *Treatise on the Law of Scotland relative to Master and Servant and Master and Apprentice.* Edinburgh: Clark

251. Steele, D.R (1843): *The Art of Sailmaking.* Reprinted 2008 Whitefish, Montana: Kessinger Publishing Co. Also www.hmsrichmond.org/sailmker.htm and Orr (1852)

252. Orr (1852) 28

253. Weir (1829) 11

254. Macarthur (1932)

255. Anon (2009) 38 *et seq* and Macarthur (1932)

256. Bowie (undated) 3

257. NAS RS54/293/267

258. NAS RS54 291/231

259. NAS SC53/56/5

260. NAS RS54/354/190

261. NAS RS54/376/15

262. Macarthur (1932) 186

263. http://numismatics.org/collection/1948.103.2

264. Trusted customers had such books in my local shop until the late 1970s.

265. NAS PR 685/264

266. NAS PR 992/253

267. NAS PR 107/49

268. NAS RS54/1094/68

269. NAS PR 185/215

270. NAS PR 903/37

271. The various amounts collected for the captains and crew were reported in several newspapers, especially the *New York Daily Times*. These notes are a 'best guess' because not all the amounts tally.

272. Twenty years later, a reporter from Philadelphia visited Robert in Antwerp and was shown the chronometer with pride. *North American and United States Gazette* September 3rd 1874

273. Taylor-Leigh (2007) 165, *Boston Daily Advertiser* April 21st 1866, *New York Tribune* XXV1 7812 1866

274. *New York Herald* June 6th 1868

275. *Providence Evening Press* XIX May 28th 1868

276. *New York Herald* July 11th 1869, reprinted in the *Jamaican Gleaner* August 5th 1869, with the additional comment that Captain Crighton was well-known in Kingston.

277. A bill of exchange is similar to a cheque, but involves three parties. A financial institution accepts one form of currency and issues the bill, requesting another institution to pay a named person or company a fixed amount in the same or another currency on or by a particular date.

278. Robert may have done this in case he did not survive the return journey, as nearly happened.

279. *New York Herald* July 17th 1869

280. Pateman (1989) 30

281. Ms Pateman had access to the Company archives, but believes she found the information in *The Bailie*, (Glasgow) of about 1879 (personal communication). This magazine began publication in 1872.

282. *Ibid* 32

283. There is a photograph of the pitcher in Crighton (1985). It was given to Arthur E Crighton by his father Robert and passed to Richard, whose second wife sold it.

284. These titles have been collected over many years by Jim Bell and latterly by me. Some of the music is held by the Levy Sheet Music Collection at Johns Hopkins University and can be downloaded from their website https://jscholarship.library.edu/

285. *Port Glasgow Express and Observer* December 11th 1909

286. *Northern Argus* April 17th 1883

287. Full transcripts of the inquiry can be found in the *New York Daily Times* from February 6th 1854. I have summarized the proceedings.

288. *Daily National Intelligencer* June 12th 1854

289. Taylor-Leigh (2007) 239

290. Stackpole (1977) 61

291. Sullivan (2008)

292. NAS RS 54/1109/43

293. NAS RS 54/1168/143

294. NAS RS 54/1181/256

295. NAS RS 54/1679/274

296. *Daily Morning News* (Savannah, Georgia) February 1st 1854

Bibliography

Anon (undated): *An account of the Rescue of Eight hundred and Fifty Passengers from the American Steamer 'San Francisco' by the British Clipper ship 'Three Bells' commanded by Capt. Robert Crighton Christmas 1853.* Private publication of which the only known copy belongs to Alan Boyd.

Anon, (2009): *From Newark to Newark: a people's history of Port Glasgow.* Port Glasgow: 7½ John Wood Street

Bowie, Janetta (undated): *The Port- Past and Present 1775-1975.* Manuscript downloadable from www.inverclyde.gov.uk

Brown, Kevin (2011): *Poxed and Scurvied. The Story of Sickness and Health at Sea.* Barnsley: Seaforth Publishing

Crighton, Richard E. (1985): *The Wreck of the San Francisco.* American Neptune XLV (1) 20-34

Crompton, Mary (2011): *A Honeymoon Voyage. A Journal of a Voyage on the SS Great Britain* (1866). Bristol: SS Great Britain

Druett, Joan (1988): *Hen Frigates, Wives of Merchant Captains under Sail.* London: Souvenir Press

Finch, V.E.W. (1988): *The Red Star Line and International Mercantile Marine Company.* Antwerp: de Branding

Gleig, George R. (1879): *Sale's brigade in Afghanistan.* London: John Murray

Hempel, Sandra (2006): *The Medical Detective. John Snow and the Mystery of Cholera.* London: Granta Books

Hirst, G.S.S. (1910, reprinted 1967): *Notes on the History of the Cayman Islands,* 5 volumes. George Town, Grand Cayman: Caribbean Colour Ltd

Hollett, Dave (1986): *Fast Passage to Australia: the History of the Black Ball, Eagle and White Star Lines of Australian Packets.* London: Fairplay

Hood, Jean (2006): *Come Hell & High Water.* London: Anova Books

Johnston, Ruth (2007): *Afterlives. Glasgow Necropolis, Tales of Internments.* Glasgow: Johnston Designs

Lubbock, Basil (1933): *The Opium Clippers.* Glasgow: Brown, Son and Ferguson Ltd

McCalman, Godfrey (1787): *A Natural, Commercial and Medicinal Treatise on Tea.* Glasgow: printed by David Niven for the author

Macarthur, William F. (1932): *History of Port Glasgow.* Glasgow: Jackson, Wylie & Co

Mone, F. (1854): *Treatise on American Engineering. Division B, Marine Engineering.* New York: Samuels, Congdon & Co

Orr, Mathew (1852, reprint): *Observations on Sails, Sail Cloth and Sailmaking.* Ipswich: Museum of Knots and Sailor's Ropework, Monograph 5

Pateman, Rachel (1989): *Wilson Watson McVinnie Ltd, 200 Years of Trading 1789-1989.* Glasgow: The Glasgow File

Smith, Robert Murray (1921) *The History of Greenock*. Greenock: Orr, Pollock & Co

Stackpole, Eduard A. (1977): *The Wreck of the Steamer San Francisco*. Chester, Connecticut: The Pequot Press

Taylor-Leigh, Tamara (2007): *Shipwreck! The San Francisco Tragedy*. LaVergne, USA: Lightning Source

Watts, Christopher T. & Michael J. (2002): *My Ancestor was a Merchant Seaman*. London: Society of Genealogists Enterprises Ltd

Weir, Daniel (1829): *History of the Town of Greenock*. Greenock: Whittaker & Co

Woodman, Richard (2009): *Masters Under God, Makers of Empire: 1816-1884*. Stroud: The History Press

Picture Credits

Frontispiece Photograph
 © Jim Bell from the cover of 'Be Cheery Boys, be Cheery'

1. © McLean Museum and Art Gallery, Inverclyde Council

2. © Reproduced with permission of the Registrar General for Scotland

3,7 © National Maritime Museum, Greenwich, London

4, 9, 11, 12 © Alan Boyd

5, 6, 8 © Robert J. Chandler

10, 14 © Christine Reich, reproduced with her kind permission

13 © Trustees of the British Museum

About the Author

Clare Abbott grew up in Birkenhead and read zoology at Edinburgh. After a postgraduate course at Sheffield she worked in information for a drug company and then for the Open University before leaving to look after her family.

In 1992, Clare inherited some intriguing family memorabilia: a portrait, a copper ring with entwined hair, a diary, letters and notes written by different people. Her curiosity was piqued and she set out to discover how she was related to the original owners of these various items. It was a task that took several years. She now helps others to find their ancestors and her special forte is to illuminate the bare names and dates with as much background as possible, using the wonderful resources, such as digitized newspapers, now available.

She still lives in the house she and her husband bought over forty years ago. Now a widow, she has two wonderful sons and two grandchildren.

Index

Abbotsford 115
Aden 18-19
Afghanistan 86, 209
Aitken, Captain James 95-96
Amelia 19-21, 94, 192
American Civil War 105, 108, 114, 202
Anchor Line 97, 98, 102
Anderson, John 187
Anglo-Persian War 86
Angra Pequena (Namibia) 15
Antarctic 31, 42, 44, 47-50, 69-70, 162, 164-165, 171, 193
Antwerp (Antwerpen) 113-118, 121, 125-126, 129-130, 141, 189, 207, 209, 213
    Police records 202, 204
    Public Library ix
Apprentice(s) 9-10, 62, 65, 94-95, 125, 135, 151, 187, 194, 206
Aquitaine, Eleanor of 2
Argo 70
Argyle Settlement (Illinois) 135, 204
Aspinwall,
    Mr G. 29
    Mr W. H. 35, 54, 174-175
    W. H. & Co 27
Aspinwall (Colon, Panama) 166
Astor House 57-58, 60, 65, 74
Auchterader 88, 125-126
Auckland 95-96
Australia xiv, 25, 45, 74, 81, 84, 86, 88, 98, 121, 129-130, 131, 133, 136, 200, 203, 210

Baltimore 127, 162, 169
Barbados 110
Barry, Major-General W. F. 110-111

Batavia (now Jakarta) 13-14, 21-22, 131, 195
Beck, William 102
Belgenland 118
Bell, Finlay 74, 167
Bell, John 97, 98-100, 102-104, 168-169, 192, 200
Birkenhead 75, 107, 113, 116, 189, 201-202
    Britannia Engine Works 125
    Flaybrick Memorial Garden 109, 126
    Rock Ferry 129
    Tranmere Rovers xv
Black Prince 105
Bombay 19, 21, 23, 86-88, 126, 200
Boston 31, 44, 49-50, 54-55, 61, 118, 134, 162-163, 165, 170
Brazil 28, 51
Brown, Sergeant Elijah R. 59, 63
Buel, Dr W. P. 29, 39, 174, 176
Buenos Ayres 25
Burgess, Amos 44, 47
Burke, Colonel 33, 39
Béliard Crighton Company 117, 189, 203

California 27, 174, 185
Cammell Laird 201
Canada 31, 74, 80, 99, 101-103, 126, 128
Cape Horn 25, 27
Cape of Good Hope 14, 19-21, 83
Cayman Islands ix, 133, 135, 140-143, 204-5, 210
Certificate
    of Competency 22, 99
    of Service 22, 131
Ceylon 86

Chandler, Second Lieutenant J. G. 41, 50, 174, 183

Chapman, Mary Elizabeth, later Crighton 117, 125

Cholera 1, 3, 30, 39-40, 44, 46, 48, 60, 176

Cingalese 13-14, 186, 192

Circe 127-128

City of New York 54, 163

Clydeside 3, 22, 103-104, 105

Coe,
    Ann Brett, later Crighton 133
    James Goodchild 133

Collins Line 49, 70

Colon (Panama) 109-110, 166

Colquhoun, Isabella, later Crighton 139, 154

Comet 154

Congressional Medal(s) xv, 110, 112, 116, 165, 167, 170

Cork 17, 22

Creighton family of Hamilton,
    Adam 141
    James 139, 141-142

Crighton,
    Adam (senior) 5, 138-140, 143-5, 154-7, 205
    Adam (junior) 5, 144, 149. 153-5, 187
    Alexander McKeich. ix, 3-7, 21-2, 131-6, 149, 170, 187-8, 205
    Alexander Thomson 105, 117-8, 127-8
    Alfred James 130
    Arthur Edward 126, 207
    Betty, see James, Betty
    Charles Edward 94, 126
    Jane see Thomson, Jane
    Jeannie (Jane) *see* McKeich, Jane or Jeannie
    John Thomson 86, 116, 126
    Kathleen 129
    Lillian Clarissa 129
    Margaret Lang, later Thomson 5, 20-2, 149, 157-8, 187-81
    Mary Catharine 108, 118, 129
    Norman Septimus 112, 130
    Robert (?1788 1828) 5, 138-40, 143-5, 154-7
    Robert (1821-1882)
        birth and childhood 3-7
        apprenticeship 10-11
        becomes master 15
        captain of the *Three Bells* and rescue, 26, 30, 41-4, 46-8
        death and burial 118
        descendants 125-130
        financial affairs 167-9, 186-9
        first rescue 22
        in America 47, 57-8, 60-70, 103-4, 110-12
        illness 71, 86, 89, 91
        marriage 22
        move to
            Govan 105
            Merseyside 106
            Antwerp 116
        personal view 120-2
    Robert (1854-1924) 74, 117, 125-6
    Timothy D. A. ix
    William (b 1795) 143-4, 149, 153-5
    William Bell 106, 118, 129, 169
    William (blacksmith) 138-9
    William Robert 118, 126, 138

Crimean War 86

Cuba 31, 133, 136

Cunard Line 49

Darwin, Charles 104

Demerara 11, 155

Derby (slave ship) 106

Deserters 76, 81

Donaldson Line 127

Dyke, William Edward 117

East India Company 18, 86, 98
Eaton, Lucia ix, 32-4, 36-7, 51, 184,
    196-197
Elizabeth 44-45

Falcon 185
Falmouth 115
First Anglo-Afghan War 13
First Opium War 17
Flaherty, Annie Clarissa, later Crighton
    129
Fleming, James 99-101, 201
Flying Enterprise xiv
Foam 33, 136
Freeman, Captain 37, 55
Fremont, First Lieutenant S. L. 59, 174-181

Gardiner, Captain J. W. T. 29, 33, 173-
    174, 177, 180-183
Gates,
    Colonel William 32, 34, 36, 38, 51-
    52, 60, 173-175, 177-181, 183-184
    Mrs 35, 52, 62
Gibb,
    First Mate 41
    John 85-86
Glasgow 22
Glasgow 3, 25, 30, 58, 61-62, 71-75, 77,
    79, 96-98, 101-105, 117, 127, 142,
    158, 165, 167-169, 190, 192, 201,
    207-208, 210
    City of Glasgow Bank 74
    Directory of (1784) 152
    Glasgow, Paisley and Greenock
    Railway Company 158
    University of 140
Gourock 153
Govan 98, 105, 126-127, 201
Graham,
    James Lorimer 57
    John Gillespie 107

Greenock 17-19, 76-77, 79, 131, 135,
    138, 143-148, 150-153, 187, 192,
    193, 206, 211
    Watt Library ix, 205
    See also Glasgow, Paisley and Gree-
    nock Railway Company
Griscom, Clement A. 113, 115
Guano 15-17, 96, 186, 195

Haiti 110, 112
Hamilton (Lanarkshire) 141-143, 192, 205
Hawaii 25
Hawthorne, Nathaniel 49
Helen Hamilton 12, 113, 192
Herald of Free Enterprise xiii
HMS Clio 16
HMS Isis 16
HMS Thunderbolt 16-17
Honduras 109
Hong Kong 18-19, 21, 24
Horsburgh Lighthouse 14

Ichaboe 15-17, 195
Illinois 135, 185
India 18-19, 23, 86, 91
Indian Mutiny 87, 98
Indian Ocean 13, 19, 82
Indonesia 13
Infants xiii, 24, 138
Inishtrahull Island 76
International Mercantile Marine Com-
    pany 113, 209
International Navigation Company 113-
    114
Ireland 12, 17, 45, 76, 104, 193

Jacob Bell 71
Jakarta *see Batavia*
Jamaica 109-110, 121, 133, 141-142,
    185

James, Betty 126
Java 13-14, 19
John Bartlet 133
John Bell 97, 98-100, 102-104, 168-169, 192, 200
Judd, Captain H. B. 36, 173, 175, 177-179, 181

Kenilworth 115
Kilby ix, 31, 38-40, 43, 51, 53-54, 69-70, 162, 164-165, 171, 176-181, 183
King Island 131
King Street 5-6, 19, 21, 131, 133, 136, 142-143, 154, 187
Kingston 110, 207
Kirk Session Records 144

Lade, James 20, 169, 187-188
Lang, Alexander 131
Laws of Oléron 2
Leguan 10-12, 192
Leila 16
Lincoln, Frederick 181
Liverpool xv, 12-13, 15, 31, 37, 44-45, 48-49, 53, 74-75, 82-83, 85-86, 88, 93-95, 97, 103, 106-109, 112, 114-118, 136, 199, 202
    Record Office ix
    Society of Friends of Foreigners in Distress 55
Loeser, Lieutenant Lucien 32, 38-39, 51-52, 174, 185
Logan, John 62
Logie 116-117
    Churchyard 117
Louisa 11
Low, Captain Edwin 38, 51-52, 54, 59, 69, 161, 163, 165

Madras 19
Malaria 14, 20, 134
Maracaibo 12
Maria (Maria Freeman) 31, 37, 54-55
Marion 131, 135
Marshall,
    Chief Engineer John 29, 35 161, 163
    Mrs 51
Mary E. Dana 127
Masonic *(Masonry)* 6, 62, 67
Massett, Stephen C. 106-107, 121
Matanzas 31, 44-45
Mathieson, John 83-84
McAlister, Helen 155
McAulay, Allan 144
McBeath, Alex 169
McDougall, William Ewing 41
McIntyre, Sergeant Tom 40, 174, 180, 182
McKeich,
    Jane or Jeannie, later Crighton 5, 131, 149, 157-8, 186-8
    Margaret 131
    Peter 157-158
McNamara, Sergeant 111
McNeil, Agnes 155
Melbourne 78-82, 84-85, 92-95, 133, 199
Mellus, First Officer Edward 29, 162, 174-175, 179, 197
Mercantile Marine Act 22
Merchant, Major 39
Mischief 20
Mohongo 70
Monken Hadley (Middlesex) 118, 125, 128-129, 203
Montreal 74, 98-99, 101-103
Mumford, Captain 199
Murray, Lieutenant F. K. 29, 36, 39, 53, 161, 163-164, 171, 174, 176
Mutiny 16, 87, 98
Mystic 110

Napoleon 31, 36-37, 45, 47, 54-55, 73, 114
New Zealand 25, 96-97
Newark (Port Glasgow) 3, 5, 209
New York xiv, 26-27, 29, 31, 44, 46-48, 50-51, 53-54, 57-64, 66, 69-73, 98, 103-104, 107, 127, 159-161, 163-164, 167-171, 173, 179, 198, 201
   Corn Exchange 161
   Custom House 185
   Freedom of 64, 161, 169
   Gold Snuff Box 66
   see also City of New York
Nightingale, Florence 197
Norfolk (Virginia) 110
North Star 55

Opium 18
   Cargo 18-19
   Clippers 210
   War 17
Orr, Mathew 152, 210

Pacific 49, 69, 84
Pacific
   Ocean 25, 82, 84
   Mail Service 27,
   South 2,
   Steamship Company 109, 112
Page, Barbara M. later Crighton 126
Palmerston, Lord 18, 86
Panama 31, 109, 112, 166-168, 185
Parker, Margaret 198
Pauline David 117
Pendleton, Captain C. 53, 161, 163
Pequena, Angra 15
Persian Gulf 86
Peru 96, 110, 185
Philadelphia 60, 67, 69, 113-116, 163-164, 169, 199, 207
Philippines 22
Phillips, Dr Charles 89-90

Pierce, Franklin 165, 173
Pirate(s) 19, 23, 29, 186
Port Glasgow 134
Port Glasgow vii, xiv, 3-7, 11, 19-22, 62, 82, 98, 118, 121, 137, 138-144, 148, 150, 153-154, 156-158, 187, 193, 209-210
   see also Newark

Québec 98-99

Rebecca 131-133, 136
Rescue 67
Rio de Janeiro 20, 27, 96
RMS Tayleur 45
RMS Titanic 2, 125
Robinson, Professor Harold R. 130
Roseanna 15, 17-19, 186, 192

Sailmaking 151, 206, 210
Satterlee, Dr R. (Surgeon) 32, 37, 176, 173, 179
Schaldis 117
Scott, Major-General Winfield 65, 173, 182
Semple, Mrs Elizabeth 140, 143, 154-155
Shaw,
   Janet, later Crighton 5, 143-147, 149, 153
   William 144, 147-148
Shields,
   Colonel 173, 182
   Senator 63
Shock, Chief Engineer W. H. 174
Singapore 14, 20-22
Snow, Dr John 40, 210
South Atlantic 20-21, 25
South China Sea 19
South Pacific 2

Southampton 125
Southworth, Mr Frederick 32, 34
SS America 49
SS Ben Vorlich 117
SS Crusader 109, 192
SS Great Britain 209
SS Mennock 117
SS San Francisco ix, xiv, 1-3, 27-29, 31-
    33, 35-45, 46-48, 50-51, 53-55, 58-
    60, 62-64, 70, 72, 81, 99, 110, 114,
    120, 126, 128, 160-161, 163-164,
    166, 171-172, 174, 176-179, 181,
    183-185, 196-197, 203, 209, 211
SS Vaderland 114-115
SS Venezuelan 109-112, 166, 192
St Helena 16, 19, 21, 88
St Lawrence River 98, 191
Stouffer, Captain 48, 50, 163, 165
Strait of Magellan 96
Strait of Sunda 19
Straits of Singapore 14
Strout, Captain 44, 55
Switzerland 118, 129
Swords, Colonel T. R. 38, 174-175
Sydney 131, 199
Symons,
    George 118, 128-129
    Madeleine Jane 129
    Terence Richard 130
    Teresa Mary 130

Taylor, Major George 31-32, 34, 63
Telegraphy xiv
Teulon, John Brown 75-77
The Wye 107
Third Regiment of the United States
    Artillery 27, 32, 50, 60, 173-174,
    176-177
Thompson, Lucy 53-54, 164, 177

Thomson,
    James 20-21, 136-7
    Jane, later Crighton 21-6, 58, 83, 86-
    8, 108, 117-9, 125, 149
    Jane and John, Jane's parents 22, 74,
    117
    John (sailor) 85-86
    Robert Alexander Crighton 126-7,
    205
Three Bells xiv, 1-2, 26, 29, 31, 41-44, 46-
    48, 54, 57-60, 62, 65-66, 69-70, 71-
    74, 84, 98, 114, 160-166, 168-172,
    176, 190-191, 192, 202-203, 209
Titan 54
Tornado 71, 74-90, 92-97, 98, 106, 126,
    192, 199
Toronto 102
Twain, Mark 67

U.S. Maritime Law 2
United States vii, xiv, 27, 38, 41, 49, 70,
    74, 107-108, 111-112, 127, 165, 199,
    202, 207
    Army 38, 49
    Artillery *see* Third Regiment of the
    United States Artillery
Uruguay 13

Valparaiso 24-25, 96
van Voast, Second Lieutenant J. 174,
    177, 179-180, 183
Venezuela 12, 110, 112
Victoria 16
Virgin Islands 112

Watkins, Captain James T. 29, 36, 38-
    39, 42, 44, 49-50, 60, 161-163, 174-
    175, 184
West Indies 6, 109, 112
Whampoa 23, 125

White Star Line 95-96

Whittier, John Greenleaf 170, 191

Wilson, Rev Benjamin Gilmore 88-93,
     121

Winder,
     First Lieutenant C. S. 49, 174
     First Lieutenant W. A. 41, 174, 179-
     180
     Lieutenant 36, 162

Wirtz, Dr H. R. (Assistant Surgeon) 33,
     173, 176, 178-180

Witty, Joseph 92, 94

Wreck(ed) xiii-xiv, 1-2, 37, 43-45, 47,
     50, 57, 60-61, 64-65, 69-70, 72, 75,
     96, 111, 120, 131, 133, 136, 159-
     160, 164-167, 172, 176, 178, 181,
     185, 191, 193, 209, 211

Wyse, Major F. O. 39, 41, 48, 59, 61-
     62, 162, 173, 176-180, 183, 185

Zarah 21-25, 83, 133, 188, 192, 195

Printed in Great Britain
by Amazon